Not Forgotten

AMERICAN WRITERS REMEMBER

THE LIVES OF LITERARY MENTORS,

FRIENDS & RIVALS

selected & edited by

Steven Gilbar & Dean Stewart

DAVID R. GODINE · *Publisher*

BOSTON

D1367831

First published in 2006 by
DAVID R. GODINE · *Publisher*
Post Office Box 450
Jaffrey, New Hampshire 03452
www.godine.com

Originally published in hardcover, in slightly different form, as
*Published and Perished: Memoria, Eulogies, and Remembrances
of American Writers* (David R. Godine, 2002).

Anthology copyright © 2002, 2006
by Steven Gilbar and Dean Stewart
*Due to limitations of space, all permissions acknowledgments appear on
pages 225–227, which constitute a continuation of the copyright page.*

LIBRARY OF CONGRESS CATALOGING-IN-PUBLICATION DATA
Not forgotten : American writers remember the lives of literary
mentors, friends & rivals / selected and edited by Steven Gilbar
& Dean Stewart.— 1st ed.
p. cm.
Originally published: 2002.
ISBN 1-56792-294-5
1. Authors, American—Biography. 2. American literature—
History and criticism. 3. Eulogies—United States.
I. Gilbar, Steven. II. Stewart, Dean.
PS135.P83 2006
810.9—dc22 2006006679

FIRST SOFTCOVER PRINTING, 2006
Printed in the United States of America

Contents

CONTENTS

[vi]

CONTENTS

CONTENTS

ELEGY, EULOGY, EPITAPH. These are all written or spoken forms used most often for memorializing the dead. They are different, not just in rhetorical or poetic style, from a standard newspaper obituary, but different by intention. An obituary is biographical and factual and nonjudgmental. Anything elegiac will raise other, deeper, concerns: the character of the individual, the meaning, impact, importance or influence of a life and the nature of memory and legacy to other generations. The elegiac, too, can be personal, even idiosyncratic, in style and content, reflecting the writer's intimate experience and feelings about the deceased and concentrating almost wholly on the personal impact of a life and death.

It was natural that the poetic and more formal eulogy would find a simpler style in what might be called the memorial or appreciation or commemorative essay. Such writing has been around for a long time; it is both secular and the product of the age of newspapers. It always seems ephemeral and fragmentary, and while such pieces may find their way into an author's collected works, the writing always displays a wet-ink, immediate, limited, and emotional character.

This commemorative essay, then, is a distinct literary form, but one without rules for content or style. Those in this book are all by American writers about other American writers, and the varieties of approach are enormously, even frustratingly, different. Why does Archibald MacLeish write so abstractly about Hemingway? The essay is good and perhaps MacLeish was trying to emphasize what he thought most important to understand at the time of Hemingway's death. But what is left out is the personal: the long friendship, battles, and difficulties MacLeish had with Hemingway. It's not there. Or take Mary McCarthy on Philip Rahv. This essay has an affectionate and emotional tone, but she is writing about the public character of the man; she never lets on that she and Rahv were lovers and you would never infer it from the essay.

The essays are always fascinating, but they have contradictory qualities. One writer will write very personally, another about character and manners, and still another critically of the subject's work. None of these essays forms, or attempts to form a suitable introduction to the life or work of the writers. That is not why they were written. They were written on the occasion of someone's death and that is what gives them a sometimes feeble, ineffable tone. Some were written in the white heat kindled by news of a writer's death; others are more reflective appreciations of a friend who will write no more.

In his essay on T. S. Eliot, Allen Tate speaks elusively of the "Thankless Muse." Certainly the commemorative essay goes unacknowledged and unappreciated by their subjects. But Tate is suggesting that a meditation on the death of a fellow writer has a kind of futility about it, and when one asks how a writer's work will be appreciated by posterity, it is truly impossible to know. Louis Untermeyer contemplates the virtues of the poetry of Sara Teasdale and notes how quickly she went out of fashion. Booth Tarkington chides the "pompous criticism" that he is sure will find fault with the work of William Dean Howells. William

O'Rourke is bitter at the neglect and misunderstanding of Edward Dahlberg. Anger is an emotion that sometimes enters these essays because anger is a common response to death, especially the passing of a friend.

There is a great silence that surrounds these little essays. They are fleeting moments of personal reflection written against the great background of time, destiny, and eternity. Yet, as a whole, they give the reader a rare look into the lives of most of the authors who constitute the canon of American literature.

Not Forgotten

Henry David Thoreau
1817–1862

by

RALPH WALDO EMERSON

Henry David Thoreau was the last male descendant of a French ancestor who came to this country from the Isle of Guernsey. His character exhibited occasional traits drawn from this blood in singular combination with a very strong Saxon genius.

He was born in Concord, Massachusetts, on the 12th of July, 1817. He was graduated at Harvard College in 1837, but without any literary distinction. An iconoclast in literature, he seldom thanked colleges for their service to him, holding them in small esteem, while yet his debt to them was important. After leaving the university, he joined his brother in teaching at a private school, which he soon renounced. His father was a manufacturer of lead pencils, and Henry applied himself for a time to this craft, believing he could make a better pencil than was then in use. After completing his experiments, he exhibited his work to chemists and artists in Boston, and having obtained their certificates to its excellence and to its equality with the best London manufacture, he returned home contented. His friends congratulated him that he had now opened his way to fortune. But he replied that he should never make another pencil. "Why should I? I would not do again what I have done once." He resumed his endless walks and miscellaneous studies, making every day some new acquaintance with nature, though as yet never speaking of zoology or botany, since, though very studious of natural facts, he was incurious of technical and textual science.

At this time a strong, healthy youth, fresh from college, while all his companions were choosing their profession or eager to begin some lucrative employment, it was inevitable that his thoughts should be exercised on the same question, and it required rare decision to refuse all the accustomed paths and keep his solitary freedom at the cost of disappointing the natural expectations of his family and friends: all the more difficult that he had a perfect probity, was exact in securing his own independence and in holding every man to the like duty. But Thoreau never faltered. He was born protestant. He declined to give up his large ambition of knowledge and action for any craft or profession, aiming at a much more comprehensive calling, the art of living well. If he slighted and defied the opinions of others, it was only that he was more intent to reconcile his practice with his own belief. Never idle or self-indulgent, he preferred, when he wanted money, earning it by some piece of manual labor agreeable to him — as building a boat or a fence, planting, grafting, surveying, or other short work — to any long engagements. With his hardy habits and few wants, his skill in woodcraft, and his powerful arithmetic, he was very competent to live in any part of the world. It would cost him less time to supply his wants than another. He was therefore secure of his leisure.

* *
*

It was a pleasure and a privilege to walk with him. He knew the country like a fox or a bird, and passed through it freely by paths of his own. He knew every track in the snow or on the ground, and what creature had taken this path before him. One must submit abjectly to such a guide, and the regard was great. Under his arm he carried an old music book to press plants; in his pocket, his diary and pencil, a spyglass for birds, microscope, jackknife, and twine. He wore straw hat, stout shoes, strong gray trousers, to brave shrub oaks and smilax and to climb a tree for a hawk's or a squirrel's nest. He waded into the pool for the water plants, and his strong legs were no insignificant part of his armor. On the day I speak of he looked for the Menyanthes, detected it across the wide pool, and, on examination of the florets, decided that it had been in flower five days. He drew out of his breast pocket his diary, and read the names of all the plants that should bloom on this day, whereof he kept account as a banker when his notes fall due. The Cypripedium not due till tomorrow. He thought that, if waked up from a trance in this swamp, he could tell by the plants what time of the year it was within two days. The redstart was flying about, and presently the fine grosbeaks, whose brilliant scarlet makes the rash gazer wipe his eye, and whose fine clear notes Thoreau compared to that of a tanager which has got rid of its hoarseness. Presently he heard a note which he called that of the night warbler, a bird he had never identified, had been in search of twelve years, which always, when he saw it, was in the act of diving down into a tree or bush, and which it was vain to seek; the only bird that sings indifferently by night and by day. I told him he must beware of finding and booking it, lest life should have nothing more to show him. He said, "What you seek in vain for half your life, one day you come full upon all the family at dinner. You seek it like a dream, and as soon as you find it you become its prey."

His interest in the flower or the bird lay very deep in his mind, was connected with nature — and the meaning of nature was never attempted to be defined by him. He would not offer a memoir of his observations to the Natural History Society. "Why should I? To detach the description from its connections in my mind would make it no longer true or valuable to me: and they do not wish what belongs to it." His power of observation seemed to indicate additional senses. He saw as with microscope, heard as with ear trumpet, and his memory was a photographic register of all he saw and heard. And yet none knew better than he that it is not the fact that imports, but the impression or effect of the fact on your mind. Every fact lay in glory in his mind, a type of the order and beauty of the whole.

*　*
*

He had many elegances of his own, while he scoffed at conventional elegance. Thus he could not bear to hear the sound of his own steps, the grit of gravel, and therefore never willingly walked in the road, but in the grass, on mountains and in woods. His senses were acute, and he remarked that by night every dwelling place gives out bad air, like a slaughterhouse. He liked the pure fragrance of melilot. He honored certain plants with special regard, and, over all, the pond lily, then the gentian, the *Mikania scandens*, the "life everlasting," and a bass tree which he visited every year when it bloomed in the middle of July. He thought the scent a more oracular inquisition than the sight

— more oracular and trustworthy. The scent, of course, reveals what is concealed from the other senses. By it he detected earthiness. He delighted in echoes, and said they were almost the only kind of kindred voices that he heard. He loved nature so well, was so happy in her solitude, that he became very jealous of cities and the sad work which their refinements and artifices made with man and his dwelling. The ax was always destroying the forest. "Thank God," he said, "they cannot cut down the clouds!"

*   *
    *

There is a flower known to botanists, one of the same genus with our summer plant called "life everlasting," a Gnaphalium like that which grows on the most inaccessible cliffs of the Tyrolese mountains, where the chamois dare hardly venture, and which the hunter, tempted by its beauty and by his love (for it is immensely valued by Swiss maidens), climbs the cliffs to gather, and is sometimes found dead at the foot, with the flowers in his hand. It is called by botanists the *Gnaphalium leontopodium*, but by the Swiss *Edelweiss*, which signifies *noble purity*. Thoreau seemed to me living in the hope to gather this plant, which belonged to him of right. The scale on which his studies proceeded was so large as to require longevity, and we were the less prepared for his sudden disappearance. The country knows not yet, or in the least part, how great a son it has lost. It seems an injury that he should leave in the midst his broken task, which none else can finish — a kind of indignity to so noble a soul, that it should depart out of nature before yet he has really been shown to his peers for what he is. But he, at least, is content. His soul

was made for the noblest society; he had in a short life
exhausted the capabilities of this world; wherever there is
knowledge, wherever there is virtue, wherever there is
beauty, he will find a home.

Nathaniel Hawthorne
1804–1864

by

OLIVER WENDELL HOLMES

I

I T WAS MY FORTUNE to be among the last of the friends
who looked upon Hawthorne's living face. Late in the afternoon of the day before he left Boston on his last journey I
called upon him at the hotel where he was staying. He had
gone out but a moment before. Looking along the street, I
saw a figure at some distance in advance which could only
be his, — but how changed from his former port and figure! There was no mistaking the long iron-gray locks, the
carriage of the head, and the general look of the natural
outlines and movement; but he seemed to have shrunken
in all his dimensions, and faltered along with an uncertain,
feeble step, as if every movement were an effort. I joined
him, and as we walked together half an hour, during which
time I learned so much of his state of mind and body as
could be got at without worrying him with suggestive
questions, — my object being to form an opinion of his
condition, as I had been requested to do, and to give him
some hints that might be useful to him on his journey.

His aspect, medically considered, was very unfavorable.
There were persistent local symptoms, referred especially
to the stomach, — "boring pain," distension, difficult diges-

tion, with great wasting of flesh and strength. He was very gentle, very willing to answer questions, very docile in such counsel as I offered him, but evidently had no hope of recovering his health. He spoke as if his work were done, and he should write no more.

With all his obvious depression, there was no failing noticeable in his conversational powers. There was the same backwardness and hesitancy which in his best days it was hard for him to overcome, so that talking with him was almost like love-making, and his shy, beautiful soul had to be wooed from its bashful pudency like an unschooled maiden. The calm despondency with which he spoke about himself confirmed the unfavorable opinion suggested by his look and history.

*   *   *

There was nothing in Mr. Hawthorne's aspect that gave warning of so sudden an end as that which startled us all. It seems probable that he died in the gentlest of all modes of release, fainting, without the trouble and confusion of coming back to life — a way of ending liable to happen in any disease attended with much debility.

Mr. Hawthorne died in the town of Plymouth, New Hampshire, on the nineteenth of May. The moment, and even the hour, could not be told, for he had passed away without giving any sign of suffering, such as might call the attention of the friend near him. On Monday, the twenty-third of May, his body was given back to earth in the placid, ancient town of Concord.

The day of his burial will always live in the memory of all who shared in its solemn, grateful duties. All the fair sights and sweet sounds of the opening season mingled their enchantments as if in homage to the dead master, who, as a lover of Nature and a student of life, had given such wealth of poetry to our New England home, and invested the stern outlines of Puritan character with the colors of romance. It was the bridal day of the season, perfect in light as if heaven were looking on, perfect in air as if Nature herself were sighing for our loss. The orchards were all in fresh flower —

> *One boundless blush, one white-empurpled shower*
> *Of mingled blossoms —*

the banks were literally blue with violets; the elms were putting out their tender leaves, just in that passing aspect which Raphael loved to pencil in the backgrounds of his holy pictures, not as yet printing deep shadows, but only mottling the sunshine at their feet. The birds were in full song; the pines were musical with the soft winds they sweetened. All was in faultless accord, and every heart was filled with the beauty that flooded the landscape.

The church where the funeral services were performed was luminous with the whitest blossoms of the luxuriant spring. A great throng of those who loved him, of those who honored his genius, of those who held him in kindly esteem as a neighbor and friend, filled the edifice. Most of those who were present wished to look once more at the features which they remembered with the lights and shadows of life's sunshine upon them. The cold moonbeam of death lay white on the noble forehead and still, placid features; but they never looked fuller of power than in this last aspect with which they met the eyes that we turned upon them.

In a patch of sunlight, flecked by the shade of tall, murmuring pines, at the summit of a gently swelling mound where the wild-flowers had climbed to find the light and the stirring of fresh breezes, the tired poet was laid beneath the green turf. Poet let us call him, though his chants were not modulated in the rhythm of verse. The element of poetry is air: we know the poet by his atmospheric effects, by the blue of his distances, by the softening of every hard outline he touches, by the silvery mist in which he veils deformity and clothes what is common so that it changes to awe-inspiring mystery, by the clouds of gold and purple which are the drapery of his dreams. And surely we have had but one prose-writer who could be compared with him in aerial perspective, if we may use the painter's term. If Irving is the Claude of our unrhymed poetry, Hawthorne is its Poussin.

This is not the occasion for the analysis and valuation of Hawthorne's genius. If the reader wishes to see a thoughtful and generous estimate of his powers, and a just recognition of the singular beauty of his style, he may turn to the number of this magazine published in May, 1860. The last effort of Hawthorne's creative mind is before him in the chapter here printed [*The Dolliver Romance*]. The hand of the dead master shows itself in every line. The shapes and scenes he pictures slide at once into our consciousness, as if they belonged there as much as our own homes and relatives. That limpid flow of expression, never laboring, never shallow, never hurried nor uneven nor turbid, but moving on with tranquil force, clear to the depths of its profoundest thought, shows itself with all its consummate perfections. Our literature could ill spare the rich ripe autumn of such a life as Hawthorne's, but he has left enough to keep his name in remembrance as long as the language in which he shaped his deep imaginations is spoken by human lips.

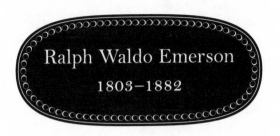

Ralph Waldo Emerson
1803–1882

by

JULIAN HAWTHORNE

THE FUNERAL CEREMONIES of Emerson were touching and eloquent, but nothing that was said or done on that occasion was nearly so impressive as was the face of the man himself as he lay in his coffin. Its austere but gentle influence was felt by all who saw it, and needed no help of spoken phrases and arguments to support its lofty assurance of spiritual immortality. There was a Roman grandeur, a serene power, in its lines and contours, that seemed to be the realization of the pure life and profound utterances of Emerson himself. The traces of weariness and uncertainty which age had begun to leave upon this countenance had now faded away, leaving only what those who had loved and studied him could recognize as the earthly symbol of his highest counsel and aspirations. That Emerson had been silently relinquishing his hold upon mortal life for some years before he finally abandoned it was not unknown to his friends. His potent spirit, which during more than a generation had aroused and illuminated the world of thought, had latterly withdrawn itself in some measure from the sphere of external activities, as if it had apprehended the imminence of a wider and freer state of vision and achievement, and wisely wished to be weaned betimes from the habitudes and preoccupations of straitened mortality. There would be inaccuracy in saying without qualification that Mr. Emerson's memory failed him. The bent of his mind was at all times so strongly toward the ideal and symbolic, as distinguished from the concrete and technical, that it is probable he never gave the latter more than perfunctory consideration, and it was not therefore surprising that he should, as it were, announce his spiritual retirement from the world by ceasing to retain in his recollection the arbitrary names of material objects. The integrity and quality of his mental structure was at no time impaired or altered, but the soul was weary of its instrument and betrayed an increasing reluctance to use it. Nevertheless those who had opportunity to engage Mr. Emerson in conversation that interested him must have noticed that the instrument soon began to respond almost as of old to the mind's impulse; the faculties, warmed into renewed vitality, showed once more their native finenesss of organization, though in a subdued and attenuated key. The most observable deficiency was, indeed, the lack of ability to maintain a consistent line of thought or argument. A topic would vanish from him almost as soon as he had ceased to speak upon it. But logical coherency, as commonly understood, has never been a marked characteristic of Mr. Emerson's writings. His essays are full of insights and expressions which are like unset gems — valuable in themselves rather than as parts of an organic design. Had he been a theorist, or in any degree an *a priori* moralist, his reputation might not have been less eminent than it was, and his traceable influence upon the philosophy of his time might have been more marked. But all that is essentially Emersonian would not have existed. For it was essential in him to seek truth for its own sake, and to accept impartially all the truth he could see, instead of making such a selection thereof as would best serve to render plausible this or that pet theory of his concerning the organization of the universe. Truth has many sides, and all students of Emerson are familiar with the numerous apparent contradictions in his writings. But it resulted from his method that Truth feared not to seek him out and make him her spokesman, as if confident that he would fearlessly and impartially give her oracles utterance; and there are to be found in his works a greater number and variety of sentences which we feel, by our instant electric acknowledgement of them, to be true, than in an equal bulk of any other writings of our time. And it is a consequence of this that Emerson, though he has many readers and lovers, has never and can never have any disciples. He enlightens, encourages, and strengthens the mind, but guides it to no definite issue or conclusion. Some of his passages have in them the germ of an entire philosophy; but they are the parts of none. It would probably be found, therefore, that he has more readers among the young than among the old. The former have as yet identified themselves with no fixed scheme of life and conduct, but are wandering afield, seeking whatever recommends itself to them as sympathetic, elevating, and beautiful. As maturity comes on, however, they gradually become committed to one or another form of doctrine, and then Emerson is found to contain much that is irreconcilable with or hostile to their prepossessions. Only a mind like his, or greater than his, could hold with him to the end; and possibly the one might be as difficult to find as the other.

*   *
*

The measure of his loss is the manifest impossibility of ever finding his successor. Who shall take the place of Emerson? His body was followed to the grave by the population of the town in which he had so long lived; and it seemed as if they had assembled to witness the interment, not of the philosopher and poet, but of Concord itself. It is hard to think of the little town without him. After Concord fight, it is Emerson that has made Concord's reputation, or rather its reputation has been he. More victorious even than the embattled farmers of a century ago, he has drawn invaders instead of repelling them. So winning were his triumphs that more than one of his most eminent contemporaries pitched their tents likewise on the banks of the lingering Musketaquid, unable to deny themselves the invigorating indulgence of his encounter. He was always accessible and always kind, but he is beyond the reach of the boldest traveller now. No one can ever take his place; but the memory of him, and the purity and vitality of the thoughts and of the example with which he has enriched the world, will abide longer than many lifetimes, and will renew again and again, before an ever-widening audience, the summons to virtue and the faith in immortality which were the burden and glory of his song.

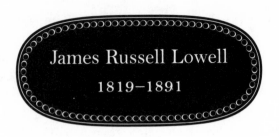

James Russell Lowell
1819–1891

by

HENRY JAMES

AFTER A MAN'S LONG WORK is over and the sound of his voice still, those in whose regard he has held a high place find his image strangely simplified and summarized. The hand of death, in passing over it, has smoothed the folds, made it more typical and general. The figure retained by the memory is compressed and intensified; accidents have dropped away from it and shades have ceased to count; it stands, sharply, for a few estimated and cherished things, rather than, nebulously, for a swarm of possibilities. We cut the silhouette, in a word, out of the confusion of life, we save and fix the outline, and it is with his eye on this profiled distinction that the critic speaks. It is his function to speak with assurance when once his impression has become final; and it is in noting this circumstance that I perceive how slenderly prompted I am to deliver myself on such an occasion as a critic. It is not that due conviction is absent; it is only that the function is a cold one. It is not that the final impression is dim; it is only that it is made on a softer side of the spirit than the critical sense. The process is more mystical, the deposited image is insistently personal, the generalizing principle is that of loyalty. I can therefore not pretend to write of James Russell Lowell in the tone of detachment and classification; I can only offer a few anticipatory touches for a portrait that asks for a steadier hand.

It may be professional prejudice, but as the whole color of his life was literary, so it seems to me that we may see in his high and happy fortune the most substantial honor gathered by the practice of letters from a world preoccupied with other things. It was in looking at him as a man of letters that one drew closest to him, and some of his more fanatical friends are not to be deterred from regarding his career as in the last analysis a tribute to the dominion of style. This is the idea that to my sense his name most promptly evokes; and though it was not by any means the only idea he cherished, the unity of his career is surely to be found in it. He carried style — the style of literature — into regions in which we rarely look for it: into politics, of all places in the world, into diplomacy, into stammering civic dinners and ponderous anniversaries, into letters and notes and telegrams, into every turn of the hour — absolutely into conversation, where indeed it freely disguised itself as intensely colloquial wit. Any friendly estimate of him is foredoomed to savor potently of reminiscence, so that I may mention how vividly I recall the occasion on which he first struck me as completely representative.

The association could only grow, but the essence of it was all there on the eve of his going as minister to Spain. It was late in the summer of 1877; he spent a few days in London on his way to Madrid, in the hushed gray August, and I remember dining with him at a dim little hotel in Park Street, which I had never entered before and have never entered since, but which, whenever I pass it, seems to look at me with the melancholy of those inanimate things that have participated. That particular evening remained, in my fancy, a kind of bridge between his old bookish and his new worldly life; which, however, had much more in common than they had in distinction. He turned the pages of the later experience with very much the same contemplative reader's sense with which in his library he had for years smoked the student's pipe over a thousand volumes: the only difference was that a good many of the leaves were still to cut. At any rate, he was enviably gay and amused, and this preliminary hour struck me literally as the reward of consistency. It was tinted with the promise of a singularly interesting future, but the saturated American time was all behind it, and what was to come seemed an ideal opportunity for the nourished mind. That the American years had been diluted with several visits to Europe was not a flaw in the harmony, for to recollect certain other foreign occasions — pleasant Parisian and delightful Italian strolls — was to remember that, if these had been months of absence for him, they were for me, on the wings of his talk, hours of repatriation. This talk was humorously and racily fond, charged with a perfect drollery of reference to the *other* country (there were always two — the one we were in and the one we weren't), the details of my too sketchy conception of which, admitted for argument, he showed endless good nature in filling in. It was a joke, polished by much use, that I was dreadfully at sea about my native land; and it would have been pleasant indeed to know even less than I did, so that I might have learned the whole story from Mr. Lowell's lips.

* *
*

I note these particulars, as may easily be imagined, wholly for their reference to himself — for the emphasized occasion they give to remembrance and regret. Yet even remembrance and regret, in such a case, have a certain free relief, for our final thought of James Russell Lowell is that what he consistently lived for remains of him. There is nothing ineffectual in his name and fame — they stand for large and delightful things. He is one of the happy figures of literature. He had his trammels and his sorrows, but he drank deep of the tonic draught, and he will long count as an erect fighting figure on the side of optimism and beauty. He was strong without narrowness, he was wise without bitterness and glad without fatuity. That appears for the most part the temper of those who speak from the quiet English heart, the steady pulses of which were the sufficient rhythm of his eloquence. This source of influence will surely not forfeit its long credit in the world so long as we continue occasionally to know it by what is so rich in performance and so stainless in character.

John Greenleaf Whittier
1807–1892

by

GEORGE EDWARD WOODBERRY

THE TIME HAS COME to pay that tribute of farewell, which is fitting in these pages, upon the occasion of the death of Whittier. The popular instinct which long ago adopted him as the poet of New England is one of those sure arbiters, superior to all academic judgments upon the literary works of a man, which confer a rightful fame in life, and justify the expectation of a long remembrance. Whittier was distinctly a local poet, a New Englander; but to acknowledge this does not diminish his honor, nor is he thereby set in a secondary place. His locality, if one may use the expression, was a country by itself; its inhabitants were a peculiar people, with a strongly marked social and moral character, with a landscape and an atmosphere, with historical traditions, legends often romantic, and with strong vitalizing ideas. There was something more than a literary fancy in the naturalness with which Whittier sought a kind of fellowship with Burns; there was a true resemblance in their situation as the poets of their own kin and soil, in their reliance upon the strength of the people among whom they were born, and in their cherished attachment to the places and scenes where they grew. New England, moreover, had this advantage, that it was destined to set the stamp of its character upon the larger nation in which it was an element; so that if Whittier be regarded, as he sometimes is, as a representative American poet, it is not without justice. He is really national so far as the spirit of New England has passed into the nation at large; and that vast body of Western settlers who bore New England to the frontier, and yet look back to the old homestead, find in him the sentiment of their past. There can be little question, too, that he is representative of a far larger portion of the American people than any other of the elder poets. His lack of the culture of the schools has here been in his favor, and has brought him closer to the common life; he is more democratic than he otherwise might have been; and the people, recognizing in him their own strain, have accepted him with a judgment as valid as that with which cultivated critics accept the work of the man of genius who is also an artist. One calls him a local poet rather to define his qualities than to characterize his range.

The New England which Whittier represents has now become historical. The length of his life carried him beyond his times. It is plainer now than it was at an earlier day that his poems are one of the living records of a past which will be of perennial interest and ever held in honor. That his early poetic career fell in with the antislavery movement was not a misfortune for his Muse; the man fed upon it, and drew therefrom an iron strength for the moral nature which was the better half of his endowment. He was, too, one who was destined to develop, to reach his powers, more by exercising than by cultivating his poetic gift; and in the events of the agitation for the abolition of slavery he had subjects that drew out his moral emotions with most eloquent heat, and exalted his spirit to its utmost of sympathy, indignation and heroic trust. The antislavery movement was his education, in a true sense, the gymnastic of his genius; but in the whole body of his work it was no more than an incident, although the most stirring and most noble, in his literary career, just as it was no more in the career of New England.

*   *
*

The simplicity and dignity of Whittier's last years, and his fine modesty in respect to his literary work, have fitly closed his career. He has received in the fullest measure from the younger generation the regards of honor which belong to such a life. In his retirement these unsought tributes of an almost affectionate veneration have followed him; and in the struggle about us for other prizes than those he aimed at, in the crush for wealth and notoriety, men have been pleased to remember him, the plain citizen, uncheapened by riches and unsolicitous for fame, ending his life with the same habits with which he began it, in the same spirit in which he led it, without any compromise with the world. The Quaker aloofness which has always seemed to characterize him, his difference from other men, has never been sufficient to break the bonds which unite him with the people, but it has helped to secure for him the feeling with which the poet is always regarded as a man apart; the religious element in his nature has had the same effect to win for him a peculiar regard akin to that which was felt in old times for the sacred office; to the imagination he has been, especially in those closing years, a man of peace and of God. No one of his contemporaries has been more silently beloved and more sincerely honored. If it be true that in him the man was more than the poet, it is happily not true, as in such cases it too often is, that the life was less than it should have been. The life of Whittier affects rather as singularly fortunate in the completeness with which he was able to do his whole duty, to possess his soul, and to keep himself unspotted from the world. He was fortunate in his humble birth and the virtues which were about his cradle; he was fortunate in the great cause for which he suffered and labored in his prime, exactly fitted as it was to develop his nature to its highest moral reach, and lift him to real greatness of soul. He was fortunate in his old age, in the mellowness of his humanity, the repose of his faith, the fame which, more truly than can usually be said, was "love disguised." Lovers of New England will cherish his memory as that of a man in whom the virtues of this soil, both for public and for private life, shine most purely. On the roll of American poets we know not how he may be ranked hereafter, but among the honored names of the New England past his place is secure.

Oliver Wendell Holmes
1809–1894

by

HORACE E. SCUDDER

THE DEATH OF HOLMES removes the last of those American writers who form the great group. This wit and poet lingered long enough to bid each in turn farewell. No doubt a longer perspective will enable us ultimately to adjust more perfectly their relations to one another and to the time, but it is not likely that there will be any serious revision of judgment by posterity as to their place in the canon. When Lowell went, Whittier and Holmes remained, and we kept on, in the spirit of Wordsworth's maiden, counting over the dead and the living in one inseparate company. Now they are all in the past tense, and all in the present; for death has a way of liberating personality, setting it free from accidents, and giving it permanent relations. Here is thus a possession by the American people which, in a paradox, could not be theirs till they had lost it; they have lost out of sight the last member of the great group, and they have gained thereby in a clearer field of vision the whole group.

The significance of this will doubtless be more measurable a generation hence than it is now, but an intimation of it is given in a parallel from the political world. We are enough removed from the great group of American statesmen who had to do with the foundation and fortification of our political order to recognize the very great interest which the American people take in their lives and their contribution to our polity. As they recede from the field of personal acquaintance they become more heroic, and stand for the great deeds and thoughts of an historic past. Research may increase the particularity of our acquaintance with their actions, but their characters are substantially fixed, and their images are formed in the minds of each successive generation; growing a little less actual, it may be, but charged constantly with greater power of transmitting the ideals for which they stood.

It is of inestimable value that the political thought of the early days of the republic should have its exponent in this noble group, and though that thought may be run into newer moulds, the characters that gave weight to the thought can never cease to have interest. But after all, general as is the political consciousness of the people, it is not so comprehensive nor so constant as is the consciousness which deals more directly with conduct, and with the whole realm of the spirit; and the existence of a great group of men of letters, appearing as it were after the political foundations had been laid, may be regarded as an event of immeasurable importance. The men whom we have been considering have made their works the entrance way to the world of beauty for a whole people, and if we take into account the probability that in a few years the great body of literature read in the public schools of the nation will be the writings of Longfellow, Whittier, Hawthorne, Lowell, Emerson, Holmes, Bryant, and Irving, we may well reckon it of inestimable moment that these writings are charged with high ideals, free thought, purity, a noble love of nature and humanity, a passion of patriotism. Nor is it of scarcely less moment that when the boys and girls who have read these writings turn to the records of the lives of the writers, they will find simplicity of living, devotion to art, and high-minded service.

A common language is essential to anything like common life in the nation. The perils which beset us now in the industrial world are largely enhanced by the lack of a common intelligence of speech. But a common literature is essential to any true community of ideals; and in the work of producing a homogeneous nation out of the varied material which different races, different political orders, and different religious faiths have contributed since the war for the Union — a work which is largely committed to the public schools — there is no force comparable to a great, harmonious literature. Therefore, for a generation to come, the spiritual host which Holmes has just joined will be the mightiest force that can be reckoned with for the nationalization of the American people.

Stephen Crane
1871–1900

by

WILLA CATHER

Iᴛ ᴡᴀѕ, I think, in the spring of '94 that a slender, narrow-
chested fellow in a shabby grey suit, with a soft felt hat
pulled low over his eyes, sauntered into the office of the
managing editor of the *Nebraska State Journal* and introduced himself as Stephen Crane. He stated that he was
going to Mexico to do some work for the Bacheller Syndicate and get rid of his cough, and that he would be stopping
in Lincoln for a few days. Later he explained that he was
out of money and would be compelled to wait until he got
a check from the East before he went further. I was a Junior
at the Nebraska State University at the time, and was
doing some work for the *State Journal* in my leisure time,
and I happened to be in the managing editor's room when
Mr. Crane introduced himself. I was just off the range; I
knew a little Greek and something about cattle and a good
horse when I saw one, and beyond horses and cattle I considered nothing of vital importance except good stories
and the people who wrote them. This was the first man of
letters I had ever met in the flesh, and when the young man
announced who he was, I dropped into a chair behind the

editor's desk where I could stare at him without being too much in evidence.

Only a very youthful enthusiasm and a large propensity for hero worship could have found anything impressive in the young man who stood before the managing editor's desk. He was thin to emaciation, his face was gaunt and unshaven, a thin dark moustache straggled on his upper lip, his black hair grew low on his forehead and was shaggy and unkempt. His grey clothes were much the worse for wear and fitted him so badly it seemed unlikely he had ever been measured for them. He wore a flannel shirt and a slovenly apology for a necktie, and his shoes were dusty and worn gray about the toes and were badly run over at the heel. I had seen many a tramp printer come up the *Journal* stairs to hunt a job, but never one who presented such a disreputable appearance as this story-maker man. He wore gloves, which seemed rather a contradiction to the general slovenliness of his attire, but when he took them off to search his pockets for his credentials, I noticed that his hands were singularly fine; long, white, and delicately shaped, with thin, nervous fingers. I have seen pictures of Aubrey Beardsley's hands that recalled Crane's very vividly.

At that time Crane was but twenty-four, and almost an unknown man. Hamlin Garland had seen some of his work and believed in him, and had introduced him to Mr. Howells, who recommended him to the Bacheller Syndicate. *The Red Badge of Courage* had been published in the *State Journal* that winter along with a lot of other syndicate matter, and the grammatical construction of the story was so faulty that the managing editor had several times called on me to edit the copy. In this way I had read it very care-

fully, and through the careless sentence structure I saw
the wonder of that remarkable performance. But the grammar certainly was bad. I remember one of the reporters
who had corrected the phrase "it don't" for the tenth time
remarked savagely, "If I couldn't write better English than
this, I'd quit."

Crane spent several days in the town, living from hand to
mouth and waiting for his money. I think he borrowed a
small amount from the managing editor. He lounged about
the office most of the time, and I frequently encountered him
going in and out of the cheap restaurants on Tenth Street.
When he was at the office he talked a good deal in a wandering, absent-minded fashion, and his conversation was uni-
formly frivolous. If he could not evade a serious question
by a joke, he bolted. I cut my classes to lie in wait for him,
confident that in some unwary moment I could trap him
into serious conversation, that if one burned incense long
enough and ardently enough, the oracle would not be dumb.
I was Maupassant mad at the time, a malady particularly
unattractive in a Junior, and I made a frantic effort to get an
expression of opinion from him on "Le Bonheur."

"Oh, Moping, are you?" he remarked with a sarcastic
grin, and went on reading a little volume of Poe that he
carried in his pocket. At another time I cornered him in the
Funny Man's room and succeeded in getting a little out of
him. We were taught literature by an exceedingly analyti-
cal method at the University, and we probably distorted
the method, and I was busy trying to find the least common multiple of *Hamlet* and the greatest common divisor
of *Macbeth*, and I began asking him whether stories were
constructed by cabalistic formulae. At length he sighed
wearily and shook his drooping shoulders, remarking:

"Where did you get all that rot? Yarns aren't done by mathematics. You can't do it by rule any more than you can dance by rule. You have to have the itch of the thing in your fingers, and if you haven't — well, you're damned lucky, and you'll live long and prosper, that's all." — And with that he yawned and went down the hall.

* * *

At the close of our long conversation that night, when the copy boy came in to take me home, I suggested to Crane that in ten years he would probably laugh at all his temporary discomfort. Again his body took on that strenuous tension and he clenched his hands, saying, "can't wait ten years, I haven't time."

The ten years are not up yet, and he has done his work and gathered his reward and gone. Was ever so much experience and achievement crowded into so short a space of time? A great man dead at twenty-nine! That would have puzzled the ancients. Edward Garnett wrote of him in *The Academy* of December 17, 1899: "I cannot remember a parallel in the literary history of fiction. Maupassant, Meredith, Henry James, Mr. Howells and Tolstoy, were all learning their expression at an age where Crane had achieved his and achieved it triumphantly." He had the precocity of those doomed to die in youth. I am convinced that when I met him he had a vague premonition of the shortness of his working day, and in the heart of the man there was that which said, "That thou doest, do quickly."

At twenty-one this son of an obscure New Jersey rector, with but a scant reading knowledge of French and no training, had rivaled in technique the foremost craftsmen of the Latin races. In the six years since I met him a stranded reporter, he stood in the firing line during two wars, knew hair-breadth's escapes on land and sea, and established himself as the first writer of his time in the picturing of the episodic, fragmentary life. His friends have charged him with fickleness, but he was a man who was in the preoccupation of haste. He went from country to country, from man to man, absorbing all that was in them for him. He had no time to look backward. He had no leisure for camaraderie. He drank life to the lees, but jested over their wine; he stood a dark and silent figure, somber as Poe himself, not wishing to be understood; and he took his portion in haste, with his loins girded, and his shoes on his feet, and his staff in his hand, like one who must depart quickly.

William James
1841–1910

by

JOHN JAY CHAPMAN

Nᴏɴᴇ ᴏғ ᴜs will ever see a man like William James
again: there is no doubt about that. And yet it is hard to
state what it was in him that gave him either his charm or
his power, what it was that penetrated and influenced us,
what it is that we lack and feel the need of, now that he has
so unexpectedly and incredibly died. I always thought that
William James would continue forever; and I relied upon
his sanctity as if it were sunlight.

I should not have been abashed at being discovered in
some mean action by William James; because I would have
felt that he would understand and make allowances. The
abstract and sublime quality of his nature was always
enough for two; and I confess to having always trespassed
upon him and treated him with impertinence, without
gloves, without reserve, without ordinary decent concern
for the sentiments and weaknesses of human character.
Knowing nothing about philosophy, and having the dim-
mest notions as to what James's books might contain, I
used occasionally to write and speak to him about his spe-
cialties in a tone of fierce contempt; and never failed to

elicit from him in reply the most spontaneous and celestial gaiety. Certainly he was a wonderful man.

He was so devoid of selfish aim or small personal feeling that your shafts might pierce, but could never wound him. You could not "diminish one dowle that's in his plume." Where he walked, nothing could touch him; and he enjoyed the Emersonian immunity of remaining triumphant even after he had been vanquished. The reason was, as it seems to me, that what the man really meant was always something indestructible and persistent; and that he knew this inwardly. He had not the gift of expression, but rather the gift of suggestion. He said things which meant one thing to him and something else to the reader or listener. His mind was never quite in focus, and there was always something left over after each discharge of the battery, something which now became the beginning of a new thought. When he found out his mistake or defect of expression, when he came to see that he had not said quite what he meant, he was the first to proclaim it, and to move on to a new position, a new misstatement of the same truth, a new, debonair apperception, clothed in non-conclusive and suggestive figures of speech.

How many have put their shoulders out of joint in striking at the phantasms which James projected upon the air! James was always in the right, because what he meant was true. The only article of his which I ever read with proper attention was "The Will to Believe," a thing that exasperated me greatly until I began to see, or to think I saw, what James meant, and at the same time to acknowledge to myself that he said something quite different. I hazard this idea about James as one might hazard an idea about astronomy, fully aware that it may be very foolish. In private life and conversation there was the same radiation of thought about him. The center and focus of his thought fell within his nature, but not within his intellect. You were thus played upon by a logic which was not the logic of intellect, but a far deeper thing, limpid and clear in itself, confused and refractory only when you tried to deal with it intellectually. You must take any fragment of such a man by itself, for his whole meaning is in the fragment. If you try to piece the bits together, you will endanger their meaning. In general talk on life, literature, and politics James was always throwing off sparks that were cognate only in this, that they came from the same central fire in him. It was easy to differ from him; it was easy to go home thinking that James had talked the most arrant rubbish, and that no educated man had a right to be so ignorant of the first principles of thought and of "the foundations of human society." Yet it was impossible not to be morally elevated by the smallest contact with William James. A refining, purgatorial influence came out of him.

I believe that in his youth, James dedicated himself to the glory of God, and the advancement of Truth, in the same spirit that a young knight goes to seek the Grail, or a young military hero dreams of laying down his life for his country. What his early leanings towards philosophy or his natural talent for it may have been, I do not know; but I feel as if he had first taken up philosophy out of a sense of duty, the old Puritanical impulse, in his case illumined, however, with a humor and genius not at all of the Puritan type. He adopted philosophy as his lance and buckler, psychology, it was called in his day, and it proved to be as good as the next thing, as pliable as poetry or fiction or politics or law would have been, or anything else that he might have adopted as a vehicle through which his nature could work upon society.

He, himself, was all perfected from the beginning, a selfless angel. It is this quality of angelic unselfishness which gives the power to his work. There may be some branches of human study — mechanics perhaps — where the personal spirit of the investigator does not affect the result; but philosophy is not one of them. Philosophy is a personal vehicle; and every man makes his own, and through it he says what he has to say. It is all personal: it is all human: it is all nonreducible to science, and incapable of being either repeated or continued by another man.

*   *
*

The world watched James as he pursued through life his search for religious truth; the world watched him, and often gently laughed at him, asking, "When will James arise and fly? When will he take the wings of the morning, and dwell in the uttermost parts of the sea?" And in the meantime, James was there already. Those were the very places that he was living in. Through all the difficulties of polyglot metaphysics and of modern psychology he waded for years, lecturing and writing and existing, and creating for himself a public which came to see in him only the saint and the sage, which felt only the religious truth which James was in search of, yet could never quite grasp in his hand. This very truth constantly shone out through him, shone, as it were, straight through his waistcoat, and distributed itself to everyone in the drawing-room, or in the lecture-hall where he sat. Here was the familiar paradox, the old parable, the psychological puzzle of the world.

"But what went ye out for to see?" In the very moment that the world is deciding that a man was no prophet and had nothing to say, in that very moment perhaps is his work perfected, and he himself is gathered to his fathers, after having been a lamp to his own generation, and an inspiration to those who come after.

Mark Twain
1835–1910

by

WILLIAM DEAN HOWELLS

I T WAS IN the little office of James T. Fields, over the bookstore of Ticknor & Fields, at 124 Tremont Street, Boston, that I first met my friend of now forty-five years, Samuel L. Clemens. Mr. Fields was then the editor of *The Atlantic Monthly,* and I was his proud and glad assistant, with a pretty free hand as to manuscripts, and an unmanacled command of the book notices at the end of the magazine. I wrote nearly all of them myself, and in 1869 I had written rather a long notice of a book just winning its way to universal favor. In this review I had intimated my reservations concerning the *Innocents Abroad.* I had hinted that six hundred pages of fun was perhaps a good deal of fun, but I had the luck, if not the sense, to recognize that it was such fun as we had not had before. I forget just what I said in praise of it, but it does not matter; it is enough that I praised it enough to satisfy the author. He now signified as much, and he stamped his gratitude into my memory with a story wonderfully allegorizing the situation, which the mock modesty of print forbids my repeating here. Throughout my long acquaintance with him his graphic touch was always allowing itself a freedom which I cannot bring my fainter pencil to illustrate. He had the South-western, the Lincolnian, the Elizabethan breadth of parlance, which I suppose one ought not to call coarse without calling one's self prudish; and I was often hiding away in discreet holes and corners the letters in which he had loosed his bold fancy to stoop on rank suggestion; I could not bear to burn them, and I could not, after the first reading, quite bear to look at them. I shall best give my feeling on this point by saying that in it he was Shakespearian, or if his ghost will not suffer me the word, then he was Baconian.

At the time of our first meeting, which must have been well toward the winter, Clemens (as I must call him instead of Mark Twain, which seemed always somehow to mask him from my personal sense) was wearing a sealskin coat, with the fur out, in the satisfaction of a caprice, or the love of strong effect which he was apt to indulge through life. I do not know what droll comment was in Fields' mind with respect to this garment, but probably he felt that here was an original who was not to be brought to any Bostonian book in the judgment of his vivid qualities. With his crest of dense red hair, and the wide sweep of his flaming mustache, Clemens was not discordantly clothed in that sealskin coat, which afterward, in spite of his own warmth in it, sent the cold chills through me when I once accompanied it down Broadway, and shared the immense publicity it won him. He had always a relish for personal effect, which expressed itself in the white suit of complete serge which he wore in his last years, and in the Oxford gown which he put on for every possible occasion, and said he would like to wear all the time. That was not vanity in him, but a keen feeling for costume which the severity of our modern tailoring forbids man, though it flatters women to every excess in it; yet he also enjoyed the shock, the offense, the pang which it gave the sensibilities of others. Then there were times he played these pranks for pure fun, and for the pleasure of the witness. Once I remember seeing him come into his drawing-room at Hartford in a pair of white cow-skin slippers, with the hair out, and do a crippled colored uncle to the joy of all beholders. Or, I must not say all, for I remember also the dismay of Mrs. Clemens, and her low, despairing cry of, "Oh, Youth!" That was her name for him among their friends, and it fitted him as no other would, though I fancied with her it was a shrinking from his baptismal Samuel, or the vernacular Sam of his earlier companionships. He was a youth to the end of his days, the heart of a boy with the head of a sage; the heart of a good boy, or a bad boy, but always a wilful boy, and wilfulest to show himself out at every time for just the boy he was.

*   *
*

Out of a nature rich and fertile beyond any I have known, the material given him by the mystery that makes a man and then leaves him to make himself over, he wrought a character of high nobility upon a foundation of clear and solid truth. At the last day he will not have to confess anything, for all his life was the free knowledge of anyone who would ask him of it. The Searcher of hearts will not bring him to shame at that day, for he did not try to hide any of the things for which he was often so bitterly sorry. He knew where the Responsibility lay, and he took a man's share of it bravely but not the less fearlessly he left the rest of the answer to the God who imagined men.

It is in vain that I try to give a notion of the intensity

with which he pierced to the heart of things, what the breadth of vision with which he compassed the whole world, and tried for the reason of things, and then left trying. We had other meetings, insignificantly sad and brief; but the last time I saw him alive was made memorable to me by the kind, clear judicial sense with which he explained and justified the labor-unions as the sole present help of the weak against the strong.

Next I saw him dead, lying in his coffin amidst those flowers with which we garland our despair in that pitiless hour. After the voice of his old friend Twichell had been lifted in the prayer, which it wailed through in broken-hearted supplication, I looked a moment at the face I knew so well and it was patient with the patience I had so often seen in it: something of puzzle, a great silent dignity, an assent to what must be, from the depths of a nature whose tragical seriousness broke in the laughter which the unwise took for the whole of him.

Emerson, Longfellow, Lowell, Holmes — I knew them all; sages, poets, seers, critics, humorists; they were like each other and like other literary men; but Clemens was sole, incomparable, the Lincoln of our literature.

William Dean Howells

1837–1920

by

BOOTH TARKINGTON

Pompous criticism will presently approach him, and, with the air of settling everything, settle nothing; for pompous criticism, which should be a science, and not an art, is neither; is no more, in fact, than the autobiography of critics, revealing their taste and education, each bit of it wearing forty masks and setting up to be the whole academy. . . .

We know what he has been to us, what he did for us, what his strong and gentle teaching saved us from doing; and in time we may be able to make it generally understood how he led the way out of a wilderness of raw and fantastic shapes where many of us dallied, making childish figures in imitation of the foolish things we found there. He was a critic, himself, indeed; not a pompous one, but one who knew how to make things and showed how to make them.

Some twenty years and more ago, when he was upon his "lecture tour" about the country, he came to a midland city where a nervous young writer, just beginning to publish, had been appointed his local courier or guide, to take him to the dinner given for him and to the church where he was to speak, and to see to his comfortable accommodation generally. No privilege could have been thought greater by the young man, who had met Mr. Howells but once before, and then under unfortunate circumstances; for the youth, a glee-club performer just out of college, had suddenly, to his own utter horror, been called upon to rise, at a Thanksgiving dinner of the Lantern Club, and sing a solo without accompaniment. Already speechless to find himself in the same room with Mr. Howells, it was more possible for him to find a voice for singing than words to decline, but the voice he found was a quavering one at a pitch nature had never planned for him, and the noises he made in his struggle were so strange that four years later, when he was appointed a day's courier for this illustrious auditor, the vocalist was still anxious to explain that the sounds had been unintentional, and the honor of making them unsought.

Of course Mr. Howells had forgotten; probably a great many people had sung to him almost as badly. He was all kindness, as he always was, and, having heard somewhere that his guide was attempting to follow the profession of a novelist, he sympathetically told him something about the pompous sort of critics, as the two drove to the lecture together in a slow little cab. What he said was not to be forgotten; nor was his kind, sad voice, a little pityingly amused, as he talked. "Ah, you'll find they can still hurt long after their power to please you is gone!" And he went on to sketch Tennyson's picture of a critic — a tiny, almost imperceptible figure in the remotest distance, no more than a dot on the horizon. "But this little, little figure, so far from you, shoots an arrow; and the arrow comes all that long, long way and finally drops down into your breast!"

To the young courier it seemed incredible that anything could strike into the breast of the man who spoke. He was our great figure in letters, secure to remain for the rest of his days dominant at the very top of possible attainment. All over the country he was an actual part of the daily life of his readers, and he had the best readers. Here and there one found a person, otherwise intelligent, who "didn't care for Howells," just as there are intelligent people who do not care for Rembrandt or George Washington, but it is safe to say that, leaving out specialists, virtually all of the intelligent readers of Howells's day are Howells readers. "All my life," one of them wrote, this winter, "I have thought of him whenever anything important happened to me, or whenever I saw anything that interested me a great deal. 'There!' I'd always say to myself, 'what would Mr. Howells think of that?' How strange it seems, sometimes, that I have never seen him! It is he who is responsible for whatever I have in the way of a mind."

*　*
*

Yet when one thinks of what he had accomplished, there is no marvel that his prodigious vigor was never lessened, but remained his when he had become an octogenarian. For, to put briefly a part of his accomplishment, he revolutionized his country's best taste in "creative literature"; he destroyed the tawdry gewgawed idols and lifted up in their place honest standards not fringed with tinsel. It was slow work; he did it patiently, without oratory, without nagging, and without invective; if he complained, his tone was tolerantly derisive. Slow, steady, and at times obscured, his revolution was accomplished by means of a growing influence which became in time the most profound and subtle that has been exerted upon the letters of his country. It is, indeed, a deeper influence than yet appears upon the surface of things, for its growth is not arrested, nor has it reached the fullness that it is destined to reach; but it is irresistible, because it offers better for poorer; therefore it will live and will have its way. There is a problem here which may be left derelict in company with another: Did he educate the readers first, and thus provide them for the authors, or did he educate the authors first and thus provide them for the readers? We abandon the question with that of the primary appearance of the hen or her egg. The great thing is that something was done.

*   *   *

Those favored people who saw the two friends, Mr. Howells and Mark Twain, together in the flesh will now often bring to mind that happy picture, for it helps to dull the smart of new grief to recall the merry moods of absent travelers, and Mr. Howells was almost always merry when he was with Mark Twain. Both their heads were white when men now middle-aged first saw them. Below the great shock of Mark Twain's white mane his remote blue gleam of eye concealed his purpose, as his voice did, until he came to the climaxing revelation it was his way to pack into the conclusion of almost every remark of his; while Mr. Howells, his perfect audience, would visibly adore each word as it slowly came, and rock and cry with laughter as noiseless as he could make it.

"The gentlest of spirits," and the wisest; thus he will be remembered. Yet there was no softness in his gentleness. His gentleness was the human kindness of a powerful iconoclast who began the overturning of the false gods.

He lived to see the fragments derided and his destructive work well on toward completion; but, more than this, his iconoclasm was not anarchic; he pulled down a poor thing, not merely to pull down, he did it to set up a better. He remembered that when half-gods go the gods should arrive, and he had the gods with him.

James Gibbons Huneker
1860–1921

by

H. L. MENCKEN

THERE WAS A stimulating aliveness about him always, an air of living eagerly and a bit recklessly, a sort of defiant resiliency. In his very frame and form something provocative showed itself — an insolent singularity, obvious to even the most careless glance. That Caligulan profile of his was more than simply unusual in a free republic, consecrated to good works; to a respectable American, encountering it in the lobby of the Metropolitan or in the smoke-room of a *Döppel-schraubenschnellpostdampfer*, it must have suggested inevitably the dark enterprises and illicit metaphysics of a Heliogabalus. More, there was always something rakish and defiant about his hat — it was too white, or it curled in the wrong way, or a feather peeped from the band — and a hint of antinomianism in his cravat. Yet more, he ran to exotic tastes in eating and drinking, preferring occult goulashes and *risi-bisis* to honest American steaks, and great floods of Pilsner to the harsh beverages of God-fearing men. Finally, there was his talk, that cataract of sublime trivialities: gossip lifted to the plane of the gods, the unmentionable bedizened with an astounding importance, and even profundity.

In his early days, when he performed the tonal and car-
nal prodigies that he liked to talk of afterwards, I was at
nurse, and too young to have any traffic with him. When I
encountered him at last he was in the high flush of the middle years, and had already become a tradition in the little
world that critics inhabit. We sat down to luncheon at one
o'clock; I think it must have been at Lüchow's, his favorite
refuge and rostrum to the end. At six, when I had to go, the
waiter was hauling in his tenth (or was it twentieth?) Seidel of Pilsner, and he was bringing to a close *prestissimo* the
most amazing monologue that these ears (up to that time)
had ever funnelled into this consciousness. What a stew, indeed! Berlioz and the question of the clang-tint of the viola,
the psychopathological causes of the suicide of Tschaikow-
sky, why Nietzsche had to leave Sils Maria between days
in 1887, the echoes of Flaubert in Joseph Conrad (then but
newly dawned), the precise topography of the warts of
Liszt, George Bernard Shaw's heroic but vain struggles to
throw off Presbyterianism, how Frau Cosima saved Wag-
ner from the libidinous Swedish baroness, what to drink
when playing Chopin, what Cézanne thought of his disciples, the defects in the structure of *Sister Carrie*, Anton Seidl
and the musical union, the complex love affairs of Gounod,
the early days of David Belasco, the varying talents and
idiosyncrasies of Lillian Russell's earlier husbands, whether
a girl educated at Vassar could ever really learn to love, the
exact composition of chicken paprika, the correct tempo of
the Vienna waltz, the style of William Dean Howells, what
George Moore said about German bathrooms, the true
inwardness of the affair between D'Annunzio and Duse,
the origin of the theory that all oboe players are crazy, why
Löwenbräu survived exportation better than Hofbräu,

Ibsen's loathing of Norwegians, the best remedy for Rhine wine Katzenjammer, how to play Brahms, the degeneration of the Bal Bullier, the sheer physical impossibility of getting Dvǒrák drunk, the genuine last words of Walt Whitman....

I left in a sort of fever, and it was a couple of days later before I began to sort out my impressions, and formulate a coherent image. Was the man allusive in his books — so allusive that popular report credited him with the actual manufacture of authorities? Then he was ten times as allusive in his discourse — a veritable geyser of unfamiliar names, shocking epigrams in strange tongues, unearthly philosophies out of the backwaters of Scandinavia, Transylvania, Bulgaria, the Basque country, the Ukraine. And did he, in his criticism, pass facilely from the author to the man, and from the man to his wife, and to the wives of his friends? Then at the *Biertisch* he began long beyond the point where the last honest wife gives up the ghost, and so, full tilt, ran into such complexities of adultery that a plain sinner could scarcely follow him. I try to give you, ineptly and grotesquely, some notion of the talk of the man, but I must fail inevitably. It was, in brief, chaos, and chaos cannot be described. But it was chaos made to gleam and coruscate with every device of the seven arts — chaos drenched in all the colors imaginable, chaos scored for an orchestra which made the great band of Berlioz seem like a fife and drum corps. One night a few months before the war, I sat in the Paris Opera House listening to the first performance of Richard Strauss's "Josef's Legend," with Strauss himself conducting. On the stage there was a riot of hues that swung the eyes 'round and 'round in a crazy mazurka; in the orchestra there was such volleys and explosions of tone that the ears (I fall into a Hunekeran trope) began to go pale and clammy with surgical shock. Suddenly, above all the uproar, a piccolo launched into a new and saucy tune — in an unrelated key!... Instantly and quite naturally, I thought of the incomparable James. When he gave a show at Lüchow's he never forgot that anarchistic passage for the piccolo.

I observe a tendency since his death to estimate him in terms of the contents of his books. Even Frank Harris, who certainly should know better, goes there for the facts about him. Nothing could do him worse injustice. In those books, of course, there is a great deal of perfectly sound stuff; the wonder is, in truth, that so much of it holds up so well today — for example, the essays on Strauss, on Brahms and on Nietzsche, and the whole volume on Chopin. But the real Huneker never got himself formally between covers, if one forgets *Old Fogy* and parts of *Painted Veils*.

*　　*
*

Here, in three words, was the main virtue of his criticism — its gigantic richness. It had the dazzling charm of an ornate and intricate design, a blazing fabric of fine silks. It was no mere pontifical statement of one man's reaction to a set of ideas; it was a sort of essence of the reactions of many men — of all the men, in fact, worth hearing. Huneker discarded their scaffolding, their ifs and whereases, and presented only what was important and arresting in their conclusions. It was never a mere pastiche; the selection was made delicately, discreetly, with almost unerring taste and judgment. And in the summing up there was always the clearest of doctrine that came, I believe, very close to the truth. Into an assembly Huneker entered with a taste infinitely surer and more civilized, a learning infinitely greater, and an address infinitely more engaging. No man was less the reformer by inclination, and yet he became a reformer beyond compare. He emancipated criticism in America from its old slavery to stupidity, and with it he emancipated all the arts themselves.

Elinor Wylie
1885–1928

by

EDMUND WILSON

THE DEATH OF Elinor Wylie hardly yet seems a real event. When people whom we know die, we have usually been prepared for their deaths by some weakening or decay of personality. But in Elinor Wylie's case, a personality still vigorous and vivid suddenly went out of being. A mind alive with thoughts and images, at what seemed its point of fullest activity, was annihilated at a stroke. In a letter she wrote me from England, just before her return in December, she told me that she had never been so happy, had never loved life so much: she had written forty poems, she said — an unusual rate of production for her. I was out on the West Coast at the time of her death, and I found that, even after the news had reached me, I kept unconsciously looking forward to seeing her in New York again. A part of my mind still kept turning toward her — for she had left New York with no farewell, but, on the contrary, with salutations and with the promise that I should see her soon.

It was true that, of recent years, she had been suffering severely from high blood-pressure, and had been warned by the doctors of the danger of a stroke such as that which actually ended her life. She had been told that, if she wished to escape it, she must diet, abstain from coffee and alcohol, be careful not to overtax herself, etc. But she paid little heed to these admonitions, and, as year followed year, used to laugh at her defiance of medical advice and her obstinate survival in spite of it.

In these latest doomed years of her life, her energy seemed actually to increase. When I first knew her, only five years ago, Elinor Wylie was a brilliant amateur, who had produced a few striking poems and started a novel or two, but who had never worked with much application. Yet by the time *Jennifer Lorn* was published, she had become one of the most steadily industrious and most productive writers of my acquaintance. She had always first composed her poems in her head and then simply written them down (in many cases, she never afterwards changed a word); but she now sat at her typewriter day after day, and turned out novel after novel, as well as a good deal of miscellaneous journalism. With a mind that seemed never to flag, she continued up to the last to go out night after night and to meet and talk to all sorts of people. In the meantime, she read insatiably. All her fiction was more or less historical and required special research. For her novel about Shelley, she collected and mastered a whole library. Her labor, in this case, was double, for she had to get up the American West in the pioneering days as well as the English nineteenth-century background. She had authority, even for her landscapes, which she would prettily rework in her own colored silks from the narratives of old books of travel. And she seemed to find time, besides, to get through all the poetry and fiction of any distinction or interest that appeared in either England or America.

It was, no doubt, partly her very abnormal condition

that so sped up her energy and imagination. Her vitality, during the years after she had come to live in New York, triumphed and flourished at the cost of desperate nervous strain. Though she had sometimes enjoyed fairly long periods of tranquillity, comfort and leisure, her life had been broken up by a series of displacements and emotional dislocations which might have destroyed a weaker nature. In Elinor Wylie's case, it had left her like one of those victims of the war who recover from critical operations and are sent out into life again, but whose condition is a little precarious. Irritation of the old wounds would at once cloud her mind with distress and terror; and one had to remember where they were. Yet in that still scarred and shaken being, who had had to live so long at the mercy of fate and under the domination of others, exasperated inescapably by the recurrent necessity to struggle, there came to birth, in these later years, what seemed to be a new and more powerful personality.

It was like the possession of a poor human life by some strong and nonhuman spirit, passionate but detached, all worldly-wise and yet unworldly, generous without devotion, ruthless without spite, laughing with unbiased intelligence over the disasters of the hurt creature it inhabited, and the mistress of a wonderful language, in which accuracy, vigor and splendor seemed to require no study and no effort and in which it spoke sometimes simply of its own divine estate, sometimes fled to bright and cooling visions for forgetfulness of its human exile, and sometimes tried to entertain by inventing the kind of tales, lending itself to the kind of sentiments, that maudlin human beings enjoy.

Such a spirit, among human beings, can nowhere find itself at home. Received in the conventional world with aversion, suspicion and fear, it creates in that other world where people avowedly live by their wits and their imaginations, an embarrassment almost equally uncomfortable. Yet the inhabitants of both worlds stand in awe of it, for they know that they must look to it for the values which they attach to the things of their worlds, for their very opinions of themselves and for their hopes of life itself. And the presence of such a spirit makes illness and death seem unreal. There are beings — and sometimes among the noblest — who pass their lives in the shadow of death. Putting all faith in the ecstasy of the senses, they cannot but fear the moment when the senses must fade: when the body fails, for them, the world ends. But for a spirit like Elinor Wylie's, death can never quite seem serious. The doctors can never dismay it. And when such a spirit drops its abode, we do not feel in its departure any pathos. Yet in its absence, we find ourselves blank: its vanishing has thrown us out more than we might have expected. It is almost as if the intellect that orders, the imagination that creates those abstractions which have come to seem to us to have some sort of existence of their own, independent of any individual — had themselves been suddenly cut off. We are here among doubtful human creatures, all quarreling or herding together, knowing little and thinking less, pig-headed, purblind and violent. We come almost to wonder at last whether that spirit has really been among us, whether it may not have been merely, like the others, a blind, violent and crippled human life. Then we remember that harsh unflurried, that harsh embittered laughter, and we look up the lively lines in the book; and we know that in this sea without harbors, our compass must still be set by such magnets as the jest and the verse.

Ring Lardner
1885–1933

by

F. SCOTT FITZGERALD

For a year and a half, the writer of this appreciation was Ring Lardner's most familiar companion; after that, geography made separations and our contacts were rare. When we last saw him in 1931 he looked already like a man on his deathbed — it was terribly sad to see that six feet three inches of kindness stretched out ineffectual in the hospital room; his fingers trembled with a match, the tight skin on his handsome skull was marked as a mask of misery and nervous pain.

He gave a very different impression when I first saw him in 1921. He seemed to have an abundance of quiet vitality that would enable him to outlast anyone, to take himself for long spurts of work or play that would ruin an ordinary constitution. He had recently convulsed the country with the famous kitten-and-coat saga (it had to do with a World Series bet and with the impending conversion of some kittens into fur), and the evidence, a beautiful sable, was worn by his wife at the time. In those days he was interested in people, sports, bridge, music, the stage, the newspapers, the magazines, the books. But though I did not know it, the change in him had already begun — the impenetrable despair that dogged him for a dozen years to his death.

He had practically given up sleeping, save on short vacations deliberately consecrated to simple pleasures, most frequently golf with his friends, Grantland Rice or John Wheeler. Many a night we talked over a case of Canadian ale until bright dawn when Ring would rise and yawn.

"Well, I guess the children have left for school by this time — I might as well go home."

The woes of many people haunted him — for example, the gag doctor's death sentence pronounced upon Tad, the cartoonist (who, in fact, nearly outlived Ring) — it was as if he believed he could and ought to do something about it. And as he struggled to fulfill his contracts, one of which, a comic strip based on the character of "the busher," was a terror indeed, it was obvious that he felt his work to be directionless, merely "copy." So he was inclined to turn his cosmic sense of responsibility into the channel of solving other people's problems — finding someone an introduction to a manager, placing a friend in a job, maneuvering a man into a golf club. The effort made was often out of proportion to the situation; the truth back of it was that Ring was getting off — he was a faithful and conscientious workman to the end, but he had stopped finding any fun in his work ten years before he died.

About that time (1922) a publisher undertook to reissue his old books and collect his recent stories, and this gave him a sense of existing in the literary world as well as with the public, and he got some satisfaction from the reiterated statements of Mencken and F.P.A. as to his true stature as a writer. But I don't think he cared then — it is hard to understand, but I don't think he really gave a damn about anything except his personal relations with people. A case in point was his attitude to those imitators who lifted everything except the shirt off his back — only Hemingway had been so thoroughly frisked — it worried the imitators more than it worried Ring. His attitude was that if they got stuck in the process he'd help them over any tough place.

Throughout this period of huge earnings and an increasingly solid reputation on top and below, there were two ambitions more important to Ring than the work by which he will be remembered: he wanted to be a musician — sometimes he dramatized himself ironically as a thwarted composer — and he wanted to write shows. His dealings with managers would make a whole story: they were always commissioning him to do work, which they promptly forgot they had ordered, and accepting librettos that they never produced. Only with the aid of the practical George Kaufman did he achieve his ambition, and by then he was too far gone in illness to get a proper satisfaction from it.

The point of these paragraphs is that whatever Ring's achievement was, it fell short of the achievement he was capable of, and this because of a cynical attitude toward his work. How far back did that attitude go? Back to this youth in a Michigan village? Certainly back to his days with the Cubs. During those years, when most men of promise achieve an adult education, if only in the school of war, Ring moved in the company of a few dozen illiterates playing a boy's game. A boy's game, with no more possibilities in it than a boy could master, a game bounded by walls which kept out novelty or danger, change or adventure. This material, the observation of it under such circumstances, was the text of Ring's schooling during the most formative period of the mind. A writer can spin on about his adventures after thirty, after forty, after fifty, but the criteria by which these adventures are weighed and valued are irrevocably settled at the age of twenty-five. However deeply Ring might cut into it, his cake had the diameter of Frank Chance's diamond.

Here was his artistic problem, and it promised future trouble, So long as he wrote within that inclosure the result was magnificent: within it he heard and recorded the voice of a continent. But when, inevitably, he outgrew his interest in it, what was Ring left with?

He was left with his fine etymological technique — and he was left rather helpless in those few acres. He had been formed by the very world on which his hilarious irony had released itself. He had fought his way through to knowing what people's motives are and what means they are likely to resort to in order to attain their goals. He was up with the best of them, but now there was a new problem — what to do about it. He went on seeing, and the sights traveled back the optic nerve, but no longer to be thrown off in fiction, because they were no longer sights that could be weighed and valued by the old criteria. It was never that he was completely sold on athletic virtuosity as the be-all and end-all of problems; the trouble was that he could find nothing finer. Imagine life conceived as a business of beautiful muscular organization — an arising, an effort, a good break, a sweat, a bath, a meal, a sleep — imagine it achieved; then imagine trying to apply that standard to the horribly complicated mess of living where nothing, even the greatest conceptions and workings and achievements, is else but messy, spotty, tortuous, and then one can imagine the confusion that Ring faced coming out of the ball park.

He kept on recording, but he no longer projected, and this accumulation, which he had taken with him to the grave, crippled his spirit in the later years. It was not the fear of Niles, Michigan, that hampered him — it was the habit of silence formed in the presence of the "ivory" with which he lived and worked. Remember it was not humble ivory — Ring had demonstrated that — it was arrogant, imperative, often megalomaniacal ivory. He got a habit of silence, then the habit of repression that finally took the form of his odd little crusade in *The New Yorker* against pornographic songs. He had agreed with himself to speak only a small portion of his mind.

The present writer once suggested to him that he organize some cadre on which he could adequately display his talents, suggesting that it could be something deeply personal, and something on which Ring could take his time, but he dismissed the idea lightly; he was a disillusioned idealist but he had served his goddess well, and no other could be casually created for him — "This is something that can be printed," he reasoned, "this, however, must join that accumulated mass of reflections that can never be written." He covered himself in such cases with protests of his inability to bring off anything big, but this was specious, for he was a proud man and had no reason to rate his abilities cheaply. He refused to "tell all," because in a crucial period of his life he had formed the habit of not doing it — and this he had elevated gradually into a standard of taste. It never satisfied him by a damn sight.

So one is haunted not only by a sense of personal loss but by a conviction that Ring got less percentage of himself on paper than any other American author of the first flight. There is *You Know Me, Al,* and there are about a dozen wonderful short stories (My God! He hadn't even saved them — the material of *How to Write Short Stories* was obtained by photographing old issues of magazines in the public library!) and there is some of the most uproarious and inspired nonsense since Lewis Carroll — the latter yet to be properly examined and edited. Most of the rest is mediocre stuff, with flashes, and I would do Ring a disservice to suggest it should be set upon an altar and worshiped, as have been the most casual relics of Mark Twain, God knows, whose three volumes should seem enough — to everyone who didn't know Ring. But I venture that no one who knew him but will agree that the personality of the man overlapped it. Proud, shy, solemn, shrewd, polite, brave, kind, merciful, honorable — with the affection these qualities aroused he created in addition a certain awe in people. His intentions, his will, once in motion were formidable factors in dealing with him — he always did every single thing he said he would do. Frequently he was the melancholy Jacques, and sad company indeed, but under any conditions a noble dignity flowed from him so that time in his company always seemed well spent.

On my desk, at the moment, I have the letters that Ring wrote to us; here is a letter one thousand words long, here is one of two thousand words — theatrical gossip, literary shop talk, flashes of wit but not much wit, for he was feeling thin and saving the best of that for his work, anecdotes of his activities. I reprint the most typical one I can find:

The Dutch Treat show was a week ago Friday night. Grant Rice and I had reserved a table, and a table holds ten people and no more. Well, I had invited, as one guest, Jerry Kern, but he telephoned at the last moment that he couldn't come. I then con-

sulted with Grant Rice, who said he had no substitute in mind, but that it was a shame to waste our extra ticket when tickets were at a premium. So I called Jones, and Jones said yes, and would it be all right for him to bring along a former Senator who was a pal of his and had been good to him in Washington. I said I was sorry, but our table was filled and besides, we didn't have an extra ticket. "Maybe I could dig up another ticket somewhere," said Jones. "I don't believe so," I said, "but anyway the point is that we haven't room at our table." "Well," said Jones, "I could have the Senator eat somewhere else and join us in time for the show." "Yes," I said, "but we have no ticket for him." Well, what he thought up was to bring himself and the Senator and I had a hell of a time getting an extra ticket and shoving the Senator in at another table where he wasn't wanted, and later in the evening, the Senator thanked Jones and said he was the greatest fella in the world and all I got was goodnight. Well I must close and nibble on a carrot.

R. W. L.

Even in a telegram Ring could compress a lot of himself. Here is one:

WHEN ARE YOU COMING BACK AND WHY PLEASE ANSWER
RING LARDNER

This is not the moment to recollect Ring's convivial aspects, especially as he had, long before his death, ceased to find amusement in dissipation, or indeed in the whole range of what is called entertainment — save for his personal interest in songs. By grace of the radio and one of the many musicians who, drawn by his enormous magnetism, made pilgrimages to his bedside, he had a consolation in the last days, and he made the most if it, hilariously rewriting Cole Porter's lyrics in *The New Yorker*. But it would be an evasion for the present writer not to say that when he was Ring's neighbor a decade ago, they tucked a lot under their belts in many weathers and spent many words on many men and things. At no time did I feel that I had known him enough, or that anyone knew him; it was not the feeling that there was more stuff in him and that it should come out, it was rather a qualitative difference, it was rather as though, due to some inadequacy in one's self, one had not-penetrated to something unsolved, new and unsaid. That is why one wishes that Ring had written down a larger proportion of what was in his mind and heart. It would have saved him longer for us, and that in itself would be something. But I would like to know what it was, and now will go on wishing what did Ring want, how did he want things to be, how did he think things were?

A great and good American is dead. Let us not obscure him by the flowers but walk up and look at the fine medallion, all torn by sorrows that perhaps we are not equipped to understand. Ring made no enemies, because he was kind, and to many millions he gave release and delight.

Sara Teasdale

1884–1933

by

LOUIS UNTERMEYER

THE DEATH OF Sara Teasdale, on January 28th, affects me so deeply, so privately, that it seems an indignity to write about her at all. Yet write I must, if only to dissipate the cloud which was flung over her during the last few years. The cloud I refer to was not her illness, for she had never been a robust person, nor was it her semi-isolation, for she never pretended to be a publicized author or even a public person. It was a cloud of prettiness which, not in the least native to her spirit, was put upon her.

When Sara Teasdale first came East from Saint Louis with a handful of clear and candid lyrics, none would have believed she would become the most popular woman poet of the decade. The early *Helen of Troy and Other Poems* (1911) revealed a self-sustaining lyricism and a blank verse that was as musical as her rhymes, but though the volume was praised, no one predicted the fervor which would accompany her subsequent books. Her work was both traditional and anticipatory. Amy Lowell had not yet published a volume; Edna St. Vincent Millay, an eighteen-year-old girl of the sea-coast of Maine, was beginning to write "Renascence," and her first book was not to be printed for another six years; Elinor Wylie was an unknown name. Within a few months, Sara Teasdale became the most loved poet of her generation; anticipating the "new era in American poetry," she became a part of it. Her *Rivers to the Sea, Love Songs, Flame and Shadow* were esteemed as highly by critics as by the casual and uncritical readers. Her unaffected quatrains, sparing and almost bare of imagery, attracted a great following. They were set to music a hundred times; they crowded the anthologies; lovers regarded the author of "I Shall Not Care" and "Spring Night" as their uncrowned laureate. A few noted her kinship to Lisette Woodworth Reese, but, almost always, she was compared with Christina Rosetti and Elizabeth Barrett Browning. One of her books (*Love Songs*) vied in popularity with *The Rubáiyát* and received the two most coveted prizes awarded in America.

In the nineteen-twenties popular taste underwent another of its unpredictable and inevitable metamorphoses. The fashion turned to keener edges, subtler byplay, a more shadowy metaphysic. Sara Teasdale was considered oversweet, over-emphatic if not over-emotional, suspiciously démodé. This was unfortunate and even ironic, for her later work is not only her most thoughtful but her best. *Dark of the Moon* is slower-paced than anything she ever wrote, more avowedly autumnal. Yet even the outspoken clarity and the flexible cadences of *Flame and Shadow*, which was the climax of her earlier work, are scarcely as compelling as the proud acceptance of change and the sombre reflections which add new dignity to the old lyricism.

This later poetry suggests, though it never reveals, the other aspect of Sara Teasdale which few, even among her intimates, came to know. It is a pity that those who knew

only the Colin-Strephorn period of her work know little of
the other self who learned French so she could read Proust,
who admired Joyce and Jeffers, and who, at the time of her
death, was at work on a dispassionate biography of Christina Rosetti and a selection of that poet's more resonant
work. Those who charged her with being sentimental
failed to realize that Sara Teasdale's quality was the trans-
lation of sentiment into sensibility, not into sentimentality,
which is only the exploiting and cheapening of sentiment
— the "professional language of emotion" as Edith Sichel
says, "without the emotion to inspire it."

Of this emotion Sara Teasdale had a surplus, but it was
emotion stiffened with austerity, even, at times, with scorn.
I had often urged her to give freer expression to this stifled
detachment — stifled, at least, in most of her work. A poem
she subsequently sent me is her answer, as well as a quiet
reproof, and since it so perfectly expresses her mature attitude, I quote it here.

My heart has grown rich with the passing of years.
*   I have less need now than when I was young*
To share myself with every comer,
*   Or shape my thoughts into words with my tongue.*

It is one to me that they come or go
*   If I have myself and the drive of my will.*
And strength to climb on a summer night
*   And watch stars swarm over the hill.*

Let them think I love them more than I do;
*   Let them think I care though I go alone;*
If it lifts their pride, what is it to me,
*   Who am self-complete as a flower or a stone.*

It is such verse that has what one must recognize as authenticity. And authenticity, rather than originality, was the gift which will, I believe, preserve a score of her simple poems long after much more pretentious work has perished. The best of her lyrics are fresh without being freakish; they are not dependent on technical innovations or the manner was not the spell of strangeness and surprise, but the more immediate and more abiding charm of recognition.

Thomas Wolfe
1900–1938

by

JONATHAN DANIELS

Some time between dark and dawn in Brooklyn or London or Berlin Thomas Wolfe once scrawled in his word-loaded ledgers a paragraph which appeared in his *Of Time and the River*. It was a paragraph which went back like so much of his writing to his undiminishing memory of things personal and things past, a memory of his father's dying in Johns Hopkins hospital in Baltimore. The roaring old man was dying without a roar, bleeding and pitiful and fragile. And Tom Wolfe who had watched with his magnificent watching memory wrote:

The great engine of the hospital, with all its secrets, sinister and inhuman perfections, together with its clean and sterile smells which seemed to blot out the smell of rotting death around one, became a hateful presage of a man's destined end. Suddenly, one got an image of his own death in such a place as this — of all that death had come to be — and the image of that death was somehow shameful. It was an image of a death without man's ancient pains and old, gaunt aging — an image of death drugged and stupified out of its ancient terror and stern dignities, of a shame-

ful death that went out softly, dully in anesthetized oblivion, with the fading smell of chemicals on man's final breath. And the image of death was hateful.

In that same hospital in the early morning of Thursday, September 15, 1938, Wolfe died and his dying so young, so far from the normal end of his great powers, makes that image of death which he saw about his dying father more hateful still. Nobody is too young to die, no gifts are so great that they hold death off. And in writing thirty-seven is not the age of infancy: if Dostoievsky, despite all his ills, lived to be sixty, and Tolstoy died at eighty-two, Byron, who died at thirty-six long outlived both Keats and Shelley. The sense of the young dying in Tom Wolfe's case comes less from his age than from the sense that he was unfinished, perhaps not yet eager to set it down. But, as Tom Wolfe, living and writing was almost a figure for the personification of Life, so in his dying he moved out of life — not in the sentimentalized terms of a minor poet who died young but as almost a legendary figure in man's ancient and unequal conflict with the grisly adversary.

Tom Wolfe will be a legend. Indeed, while he lived in his great body and in his huge all-touching existence as well as in his big books, he seemed sometimes less a man making fiction than a giant marching in his own legend which was also the legend of his people. And that story of the Gants and the Pentlands at its worst and best grew from this American earth and the people who lived upon it. North Carolina, where both Wolfe and his legend began, did not readily appreciate that. Indeed, in some quarters the relationship was resisted. In his lifetime his books were banned from the library of his native town of Asheville which in time's own irony came proudly to claim him after he was dead. That is an old custom.

But it is not only old custom. There is the custom of mourning the loss of something that never existed. Something of the homefolks' first resistance to the book about the home town may lie behind the criticism of Wolfe's books as undisciplined and formless. I suspect in some such criticism a wish, like Asheville's, to have the native story a little nicer, a trifle neater, more ordered and patterned in delicacy and decorum. And now at his death I expect that the suggestion will be strenuously stirred that had he lived Tom Wolfe's big, sprawling, powerful, pouring prose would have been served in neater packages of sweeter stuff. It is possible to say anything about the dead. In Wolfe's case, they may even make him a classicist who might have been. But our loss will remain the unbounded vitality, the uncaptured power which made his books and his words and all his Gants and Pentlands alive. Form and discipline undoubtedly in important respects he lacked; it is lacking also in the confusion which is as much a part of American life as Tom Wolfe was.

In the truest sense he was the American wanderer — footloose, headloose, heartloose — even if his frontiers were Harvard and Brooklyn. He moved under the stars and the sun and somehow moving, he was the Paul Bunyan of the heart and mind. He left his native North Carolina early; the years of his writing were spent outside of it. But never was a State carried so far and so completely as in the writing memory of this son. As he knew it he set it down in love, in contempt, in beauty and in ugliness. In no other writing has an American State been so passionately, so sensitively, so sharply drawn. Ultimately it was a portrayal full of love shaped far off in a strange nostalgia for place and people which was nowhere blinded by sentiment or blurred by the softening quality of distance. He drew his land as it was and wise men in it rejoiced for the drawing.

Men in his homeland honored him for his work. The last anger disappeared. When he went back last year hostility turned into hospitality, and for Wolfe, who had little self-protective power, the hospitality was sometimes more destructive than the hostility could have been. There was suggestion that he planned to come back to the North Carolina mountains to live and work. The sense that he belonged to North Carolina seemed to be growing both in Wolfe and in the State. Well, that is finished now: there will be no homecoming nor welcome now. Only a body went home, home to the hills of the Pentlands, home to the Altamont of the Gants. But it went properly home to his earth. Restless and wandering as Tom Wolfe was in his living, the chance is that he would have been restless and unhappy dead in any earth but his own.

His people have received the man as he was — and he was not easy for he was a strange one among them. The book folk will have an easier task. They may accept him and miss him for what he was — as formless, as undisciplined as the American story and as hungry and boisterous as the American in it. Or they may weep for a Tom Wolfe who might have emerged some time as something different, disciplined and precise. Wolfe's work, full of fault maybe but full of riches, too, is Wolfe. The man who might have been is an irrelevant phantom. We have loss enough to mourn.

F. Scott Fitzgerald
1896–1944

by

JOHN O'HARA

IT IS GRANTED that Scott Fitzgerald was not a lovable
man, but most of the time he was a friendly one, and that
characteristic, in a man of his professional standing, is as
much as anyone can ask. I always warmed to Scott, was
always glad to see him, always. But then if you saw him too
long a time his intelligence, about which he was almost
overconscientious, would go to work, and he would let you
bore him. He would almost encourage you to bore him. He
let you go right ahead, being banal and uninteresting, and
knowing how much you were embarrassed yourself by
your ordinariness. At the same time he was professionally
one of the most generous artists I've ever known. Dorothy
Parker pointed that out to me one time when I had some
reason to be irritated with Scott, and though Dorothy
Parker has said many true things, she has said nothing
truer than that. I guess the loneliness of his private hells
was so enormous that he really would have got no great
relief by sharing a little of it — in other words, by letting
you know him better — and so figured to keep it all for
himself. Well, that was his business, and thus he kept his

integrity, which I won't attempt to define, simply because everyone who knew him knew he had it.

And he kept it in death. I read the *Herald Tribune* obit and I understand the *Times* one was just as bad. The curious hostility of those pieces may be attributed to that integrity coming through, even to people who didn't know Scott, who probably hadn't even read him (I am reliably informed that the piece in *Time* was written by a man who until he was assigned to do the piece never had read anything of Scott's). The integrity, the aloofness, came through and annoyed some people, and so they just went ahead and wrote their angry little pieces, saving their wit and tolerance for some spectacular Bowery bum or deputy chief inspector of police.

F. Scott Fitzgerald was a *right* writer, and it's going to be a damned shame if the generation after mine (I am thirty-six) and the one after that don't get to know him. I had the good luck to read *This Side of Paradise* when it first came out, twenty years ago, and I've read it practically annually since then. He was the first novelist to make me say, "Hot dog! Some writer, I'll say." I was younger than his people in *This Side of Paradise*, but I was precocious. Amory Blaine's mother's maiden name was Beatrice O'Hara, and I was in love with a girl name Beatrice then, a coincidence that became less important page by page. The people were right, the talk was right, the clothes, the cars were real, and the mysticism was a kind of challenge. By the time *The Beautiful and the Damned* and *The Great Gatsby* appeared, the man could do no wrong. In a burst of enthusiasm I once said to Dorothy Parker, "The guy just can't write a bad piece." And again she was right. She said, "No. He can write a bad piece, but he can't write badly." He sent me the page proofs

of *Tender Is the Night,* which was a major honor in my life.
I read it three times then, but only twice since, for that fine
book is not to be read just any time. It's a dangerous book
to encounter during some of the moods that come over
you after you're thirty. You don't like to think of yourself,
lone, wandering and lost, like Richard Diver, going from
town to town in bleak upstate New York, with All That
behind you.

And then a year ago Scott invited us out to his house in
the San Fernando Valley for Sunday lunch. It was going to
be a big thing, though a small party. He was going to have
Norma Shearer and Loretta Young, and I wish I had told
him that if I were choosing people to lunch with I would
not pick either Norma Shearer and/or Loretta Young. Anyway, they weren't there. There were only my wife and I.
The food was good and there was a lot to drink, but I was
on the wagon and Scott was not. He was terribly nervous,
disappearing for five and ten minutes at a time, once to get
a plaid tie to give my wife because she was wearing a Glen
plaid suit. Once to get a volume of Thackeray because I'd
never read Thackeray, another time to get some tome
about Julius Caesar which he assured me was scholarly but
readable — but which he knew I would never read. Then
we went out and took some pictures, and when we finished
that he suddenly said, "Would you like to read what I've
written, but first promise you won't tell anyone about it.
Don't tell them anything. Don't tell them what it's about,
or anything about the people. I'd like it better if you didn't
even tell anyone I'm writing another novel." So we went
back to the house and I read what he had written. He saw
that I was comfortable, with pillows, cigarettes, ash trays,
a Coke. And sat there tortured, trying to be casual, but

unhappy because he did not know that my deadpan was partly due to my being an extremely slow reader of good writing, and partly because this *was* such good writing that I was reading. When I had read it I said, "Scott, don't take any more movie jobs till you've finished this. You work so slowly and this is so good, you've got to finish it. It's real Fitzgerald." Then, of course, he became blasphemous and abusive, and asked me if I wanted to fight. I saw him a few times after that day, and once when I asked him how the book was coming he only said, "You've kept your promise? You haven't spoken to anyone about it?"

Sherwood Anderson
1876–1941

by

THEODORE DREISER

Anderson, his life and his writings, epitomize for me the
pilgrimage of a poet and a dreamer across this limited
stage called Life, whose reactions to the mystery of our
being and doings here (our will-less and so wholly auto-
matic responses to our environing forces) involved tenderness, love and beauty, delight in the strangeness of our
will-less reactions as well as pity, sympathy and love for all
things both great and small. Whenever I think of him I
think of that wondrous line out of "The Ancient Mariner"
— "He prayeth best who lovest best all things both great
and small." And so sometimes the things he wrote, as well
as the not too many things he said to me personally, had
the value of a poetic prayer for the happiness and the well-
being of everything and everybody — as well as the well-
outcoming of everything guided as each thing plainly is by
an enormous wisdom — if seemingly not always imbued
with mercy — that none-the-less "passeth all understanding." He seemed to me to accept in humbleness, as well as
in and of necessity in nature, Christ's dictums "The rain
falleth on the just and unjust." Also that we are to "Take
no thought for your life, what ye shall eat, or what ye shall

[77]

drink nor yet for your body, what ye shall put on. Is not the life more than meat, and the body than raiment?"

As I see him now there was something Biblical and prophetic about him. Through all his days he appears to have been wandering here and there, looking, thinking, wondering. And the things he brought back from the fields of life! *Dark Laughter, Many Marriages, The Triumph of the Egg, Midwestern Chants, Winesburg,* — in which is that beautiful commentary on the strain of life on some temperaments called "Hands". It is to me so truly beautiful, understanding and loving, and weeping, almost, for the suffering of others.

Well he is gone — wise, kind, affectionate, forgiving. And I wish he were not. To me, amidst all the strain of living and working, he was a comforting figure — never in any sense a slave to money, or that other seeming necessity to so many, show, or pretense. He was what he was and accepted himself in just that sense — "I am what I am." — "Take me or leave me for what I am to you." And I, like millions of others, I am sure, have taken him in just that sense. And other millions will, I feel, for the duration at least of our American literature.

Ernie Pyle
1900–1944

by

RANDALL JARRELL

H E WROTE like none of the rest. The official, press-agent, advertising-agency writing that fills the newspapers, magazines, and radio with its hearty reassuring lies, its mechanical and heartless superlatives; the rhetorical, sensational, and professional pieces of ordinary TimeLife journalism — the same no matter what the subject, who the writer; the condescending, preoccupied work of "real writers" officially pretending to be correspondents for the duration: all this writing about the war that by its quality denies the nature and even the existence of the war, he neither competed with nor was affected by. He was affected by, obsessed with, one thing — the real war: that is, the people in it, all those private wars the imaginary sum of which is the public war; and he knew that his private war, his compulsive obligation, was to write what he had seen and heard and felt so that neither those who had felt it nor those who had not could ever again believe that it was necessary for anyone to be ignorant of it. He was their witness; and he looked not to find evidence for his own theories or desires, to condemn, to explain away, to justify, but only to see and to tell what he saw! What he cared about was the facts. But facts are only facts as we see them, as we feel them; and he knew to what a degree experience — especially in war — is "seeing only faintly and not wanting to see at all." The exactly incongruous, the crazily prosaic, the finally convincing fact — that must be true because no one could have made it up that must be Pyle because no one else would have noticed it — was his technical obsession, because he knew it was only by means of it that he could make us understand his moral obsession: what happens to men in our war. (A few reporters cared almost as much and tried almost as hard; but their work is hurt by emotional forcing, self-consciousness, the hopeless strain between their material and their technique. To the reporter's trained consciousness there is something incidental, merely personal, almost meretricious, about his exact emotions or perceptions or moral judgments; these things are not part of "the facts," and he professionally supplies only as much of their generalized, familiar equivalents as his readers immediately demand and immediately accept. These things, for many years, had been the only facts for Pyle.) Pyle did not care how he told it if he could make us feel it; there is neither self-protectiveness nor self-exploitation in his style. What he saw and what he felt he said. He used for ordinary narration a plain, transparent, but oddly personal style — a style that could convince anybody of anything; but when his perceptions or emotions were complex, far-reaching, and profound, he did his utmost to express their quality fully — at his best with the most exact intensity, at his worst with a rather appealingly old-fashioned spaciousness of rhetoric. It is easy to be critical of some of these last passages, and of the flat homeliness of others: he possessed few of the unessential qualities of the accomplished writer

but — at his rare best — many of the essential qualities of
the great writer. It was puzzling and disheartening to read
some of the reviews of his books: the insistence that this
was not "great" reporting, the work of a "real" writer, but
only a good reporter, a good man — nobody missed that —
reproducing what the "G.I. Joes" felt and said. (Some writers seemed compelled to use about him, as they do about all
soldiers who are at the same time enlisted men, the words
simple, plain, or little — so disquieting in their revelation
of the writers' knowledge and values.) And yet all of us
knew better. We felt most the moral qualities of his work
and life; but we could not help realizing that his work was,
in our time, an unprecedented aesthetic triumph: because
of it most of the people of a country felt, in the fullest
moral and emotional sense, something that had never happened to them, that they could never have imagined without it — a war.

In war the contradictions of our world, latent or overt,
are fantastically exaggerated; and what in peace struggles
below consciousness in the mind of an economist, in war
wipes out a division on atolls on the other side of a planet.
So in Pyle war is the nest of all contradictions; the incongruous is the commonplace homogeneous texture of all
life. All of them know it: a cannoneer, playing poker by two
candles in a silent battery, says to him "as though talking in
his sleep. 'War is the craziest thing I ever heard of.'" A man
builds a raft to float on the water of his foxhole; another
goes to sleep, falls over in the water, and wakes up, until he
finally ties himself by a rope to a tree; four officers of a tank
company fix themselves a dugout with electric lights, a pink
stove, an overstuffed chair, and "a big white dog, slightly
shell-shocked, to lie on the hearth." Men in shallow fox-

holes, under severe strafing, try to dig deeper with their fingernails, are commonly "hit in the behind by fly; fragments from shells. The medics there on the battlefield would either cut the seats out of their trousers or else slide their pants down, to treat the wounds, and they were put on the stretchers that way, lying face down. It was almost funny to see so many men coming down the hill with the white skin of their backsides gleaming against the dark background of brown uniforms and green grass." Pyle "couldn't help feeling funny about" fighter pilots who had just strafed a truck convoy, and who, "so full of laughter . . . talked about their nights and killing and being killed exactly as they would discuss girls or their school lessons." Soldiers pile out of their jeeps for an approaching bird, thinking it a Stuka ("I knew one American outfit that was attacked by Stukas twenty-three times in one day. A little of that stuff goes a long way"); and a digger testifies, with utter magnificence: "Five years ago you couldn't have got me to dig a ditch for five dollars an hour. Now look at me. You can't stop me digging ditches. I don't even want pay for it; I just dig for love. And I sure do hope this digging today is all wasted effort, I never wanted to do useless work so bad in all my life. Any time I get fifty feet from my home ditch you'll find me digging a new ditch and, brother, I ain't joking. I love to dig ditches." And yet it is a war where "few ever saw the enemy, ever shot at him, or were shot at by him"; where "physical discomfort becomes a more dominant thing in life than danger itself"; where everything is so scarce that passing soldiers stop Pyle six times in a day to borrow a pair of scissors to cut their nails — "if somebody had offered me a bottle of castor oil I would have accepted it and hidden it away."

Pyle is always conscious of the shocking disparity of actor and circumstance, of the little men and their big war, their big world: riding in a truck in the middle of the night, so cold he has to take off his shoes and hold his toes in his hands before he can go to sleep, he feels shiveringly "the immensity of the catastrophe that had put men all over the world, millions of us, to moving in machine-like precision through long nights — men who should have been comfortably asleep in their warm beds at home. War makes strange giant creatures out of us little routine men that inhabit the earth." And, flying from the Anzio beachhead to D-Day in the Channel, passing at sunset over the peaks of the Adas, he thinks longingly of the worlds inside the world: "Down below lived sheep men — obscure mountain men who had never heard of a Nebelwerfer or a bazooka, men at home at the end of the day in the poor, narrow, beautiful security of their own walls." His column describing the apotheosis of another world, the debris of the Normandy beachhead, is so extraordinary in its sensitivity, observation, and imagination that I wish I could quote all of it; but, taken at random from "this long thin line of personal anguish": from the sleeping, dead, and floating men; from the water "full of squishy little jellyfish . . . in the center of each of them a green design exactly like a four-leaf clover"; from the ruined tanks, trucks, bulldozers, half-tracks, typewriters, office files, steel matting, and oranges, a banjo and a tennis racket; from the dogs, Bibles, mirrors, cigarette cartons (each soldier was given a carton of cigarettes before embarking), and writing paper of that universe where "anything and everything is expendable," here are two objects:

I stooped over the form of one youngster whom I thought dead. But when I looked down I saw that he was only sleeping. He was very young, and very tired. He lay on one elbow, his hand suspended in the air about six inches from the ground. And in the palm of his hand he held a large, smooth rock.

I stood and looked at him for a long time. He seemed in his sleep to hold that rock lovingly, as though it were his last link with a vanishing world. . . .

As I plowed out over the wet sand, I walked around what seemed to be a couple of pieces of driftwood sticking out of the sand. But they weren't driftwood. They were a soldier's two feet. He was completely covered except for his feet; the toes of his G.I. shoes pointed toward the land he had come so far to see, and which he saw so briefly.

*　　*

*

He was very much more complex than most people suppose; and his tragedy — a plain fatality hung over the last of his life, and one is harrowed by his unresigned I've used up my chances — was not at all that of the simple homogeneous nature destroyed by circumstances it is superior to. People notice how well he got along with people and the world — and talk as if he were the extrovert who naturally does so; actually he was precisely, detailedly, and unremittingly introspective and the calm objectivity of his columns is a classical device — his own confused and powerful spiritual life always underlies it, and gives it much of its effect. This contradictory struggle between his public and private selves, between the controlled, objective selectivity of the pieces and his own intense inner life, one must guess from fragments or the remarks of those who knew him best; it is partly because this one side of him is incompletely represented in his work that one regrets his death so much.

His writing, like his life, is a victory of the deepest moral feeling of sympathy and understanding and affection, over circumstances as terrible as any men have created and endured. By the veneration and real love many millions of people felt for him, their unexplained certainty that he was different from all the rest, and theirs, they showed their need and gratitude for the qualities of his nature, and seemed almost to share in them. He was a bitter personal loss for these people. Most of his readers could not escape the illusion that he was a personal friend of theirs; actually he was — we meet only a few people in our lives whom we ever know as well or love as much. There are many men whose profession it is to speak for us — political and military and literary representatives of that unwithering estate which has told us all our lives what we feel and what we think, how to live and when to die; he wrote what he had seen and heard and felt himself, and truly represented us. Before his last landing in the Ryukyus, he felt not only fear and revulsion but an overwhelming premonition that he would die there: "repeatedly he said he knew he would be killed if he hit another beachhead. Before he finally settled the question of whether or not to go ashore in his own mind, he spent three sleepless days and nights. Then on the fourth day he made up his mind." He told a good friend, "Now I feel all right again"; to other people he said merely that he didn't want to go there, but he guessed the others didn't either. He had to an extraordinary degree the sense of responsibility to the others, the knowledge of his own real duty, that special inescapable demand that is made — if it is made — to each of us alone. In one sense he died freely, for others; in another he died of necessity and for himself. He had said after visiting the lepers in the Hawaiian Islands: "I felt a kind of unrighteousness at being whole and 'clean.' I experienced an acute feeling of spiritual need to be no better off than the leper."

After he died I saw, as most people did, a newsreel of him taken in the Pacific. He is surrounded by Marines trying to get his autograph, and steadies on the cropped head of one of them the paper he is signing. He seems unconscious of himself and the camera; his face is humorous, natural, and kindly, but molded by the underlying seriousness, almost severity, of private understanding and judgment. I remembered what the girl in *The Woodlanders* says over another grave: "You were a good man and did good things." But it is hard to say what he was or what we felt about him. He filled a place in our lives that we hardly knew existed, until he was there; and now that he is gone it is empty.

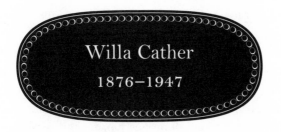

Willa Cather
1876–1947

by

HENRY SEIDEL CANBY

AMONG THE NOVELISTS who reached their height of achievement in the twenties was Willa Cather, whose death on April 24 ends a great career in American literature. She had already, before the twenties, shown what Americans could do with the rich experience of pioneer life. A personable woman, of finely cut features, with a delicate flush which deepened when ideas warmed her imagination, she was definitely an intellectual aristocrat. She had a way of summoning you to a tea or a conference which proved not the less stimulating because commanded. Actually, as one soon found out, she was guarding her working hours and working energy. She had a fierce devotion to her art which was not vanity, but came from a clearer view than that of most of her contemporaries of the difficulty of achieving even a relative perfection. You can read about it, written of others but applicable to herself, in a book of her essays called *Not Under Forty.*

Willa Cather's mind had the precision of a scholar's, the penetration of a critic's, and the warm intellectuality of a creative artist's. She had led an active editorial life on the staff of the old *McClure's,* which had put the vitality of new

European minds and the audacity of the American muck-rakers into a cheap and readable magazine just when the genteel periodicals were going stale. It could be tough; it was sensational; respectable editors regarded it as a por-tent of vulgarity — which only shows that the vulgarity of one generation may prove to be the respectable realism of another. She had done her job in the literary, not the muckraking department, and had wholeheartedly retired into the art of fiction.

As we sat talking, she would ask me the news of that old editorial world; what had happened as a result of this or that, or where were the old fighters now and what were they doing. I could only reply that I lived in an ivory tower in those days and did not know the answers. But this was an introduction to our real talk. Miss Cather was one of the few writers I have known who passionately desired to talk of the craft of good writing with only the most indirect reference to her own work. In this she had what I should call a Gallic mind. The subject matter of her most impor-tant books was taken from what was most vital in American pioneer experience, yet the tradition of her craftsmanship was certainly French. The name of Flaubert was often on her lips. She had the most uncommon passion for perfection — but what she liked to analyze as we talked was what constituted perfection for a given situation or a theme. This is French rather than English or American, and when pur-sued in writing by an Englishman or an American often leads to artificiality. Not so with her. She wished to know how the great ones achieved, not to imitate them. Her idea was that the consummate artist in fiction gave himself entirely to the situation he chose for his story, following its nuances, not shaping it to preconceived effects. That was what she wanted to talk about; what she did herself in *O Pioneers!* and *Death Comes for the Archbishop.*

Not long ago I sat with Miss Cather at a meeting of the National Institute of Arts and Letters, at which she was to be given the gold medal in fiction, their highest honor. She had been ill, her face was drawn, her pace a little unsteady. That day a special award for lifetime service was given to Samuel McClure, then well into his eighties. When he was helped to the platform, the color came back to her cheek, and, with the warm impulsiveness one finds always in her best heroines, she ran forward and kissed and embraced him. I do not suppose that Willa Cather was the greatest American novelist of the 1910s and '20s, bigness was not her metier — that she left to the Upton Sinclairs, who had less art. Certainly she was the most skilful, and one of the best.

Edna St. Vincent Millay
1892–1950

by

ROLFE HUMPHRIES

SHE WAS FOUND lying dead alone at the foot of the stairs; and since then, it seems, everybody — except one or two boors who saw fit to kick her — has been stepping over her, ever so delicately, as if the remembered twenties, hers, ours, and the century's, were something rather embarrassing in view of the spacious and enlightened times to which we survivors have now progressed

What stuff and nonsense! What dreadful cant!

She wrote some bad verse when she was young, and some worse verse when she was older, as who has not, witness John Keats at one end and William Wordsworth at the other. She could be silly, cute, arch, hysterical; she could commit ghastly errors of taste. She also could, and did, write so memorably that her language was on every tongue. Her currency, her circulation, wore down her coinage to counters. So she was vogue, and now she is dated. They say.

Tease not her ghost with slander. She was a fine lyric poet, also, in the classical sense, a fine elegiac poet, and the dates of her *floruit* matter as little as Sulpicia's or Sappho's. She expressed a great deal more than the spirit of a tinsel age: there was silver of an individual voice, the legal tender of no base emotion. She could feel, and she could put into words; there was wit there, and clarity, mastery of epithet, control of modulation. Like Housman, whom it is also fashionable to deplore, she composed her own music out of old ballad airs and the clear ringing Latin that she loved. She had an ear; and that gift is not a trinket which can be comfortably hidden away in the bureau drawer of a decade.

We have no one like her today, when a "young" poet is somebody around the age of forty, with the trite vocabulary of his particular camp and a spirit fatigued by the banalities of its particular campaigns. In her youth she had two qualities, neither too common — an immediately individual style and a capacity for ecstasy. I do not mean that word in the sense in which it is misused, oh, so often, by ladies who write poems, but in its true Greek sense of standing outside the self. Whereto, whatever its gaucheries, the poem "Renascence" bore witness.

But it was not only in the first fine careless rapture that her excellence was found. The ardor was chastened, but the lyric quality persisted, graver, more reflective, a little sorrowful for being wiser, a good deal subtler as the rhythms were moved to the more pensive mood. Never cited as characteristic, half a dozen lyrics, at least, from *The Buck in the Snow* volume: "Song", "The Hardy Garden", the title poem, "To a Young Girl", "Evening on Lesbos", "The Cameo", "Counting-out Rhyme" — all these, did they come to us new today, would mark a talent of distinction.

*   *
*

Almost everybody can write sonnets that sound like almost everybody else's; hers did not, and she wrote many. Her skill with the form led her on to risk the challenge of the sonnet sequence, than which only the sestina offers a quicker and surer bid to dulness. Neither of her sequences, the "Epitaph for the Race of Man" and the "Fatal Interview," could be labeled dull, though there were moments of embarrassment; the texture might be frayed or ravel out, but there always was a texture. And there was some very lovely weaving — "Moon that against the lintel of the west," or "O sleep forever in the Latmian cave"; enjoyment might differ, with the individual, in response to this or that number. But all of us, I hope, could consent and agree in delight with

> *Not in a silver casket cool with pearls*
> *Or rich with red corundum or with blue,*
> *Locked, and the key withheld, as other girls*
> *Have given their loves, I give my love to you;*
> *Not in a lovers'-knot, not in a ring*
> *Worked in such fashion, and the legend plain —*
>
> Semper fidelis, *where a secret spring*
> *Kennels a drop of mischief for the brain:*
> *Love in the open hand, no thing but that,*
> *Ungemmed, unhidden, wishing not to hurt,*
> *As one should bring you cowslips in a hat*
> *Swung from the hand or apples in her skirt,*
> *I bring you, calling out as children do:*
> *"Look what I have! — And these are all for you."*

Tease not her ghost with slander.

Wallace Stevens
1879–1955

by

DELMORE SCHWARTZ

THE DEATH OF Wallace Stevens concludes one of the most extraordinary of poetic careers. It is difficult to speak of the death of any human being without soon being overcome by the conviction that silence is the only appropriate speech. When it is the death of a great poet — a very great poet — comments seems inadequate and gratuitous. Perhaps it would be best to describe one of his rare public appearances.

In 1936 Stevens read his poems for the first time at Harvard — it was probably the first time he had ever read his poetry in public — and the occasion was at once an indescribable ordeal and a precious event: precious because he had been an undergraduate and a poet at Harvard some thirty-seven years before and had not returned since then, in his own person, although he had often gone to the Yale-Harvard games incognito. Before and after reading each poem, Stevens spoke of the nature of poetry, a subject which naturally obsessed him: the least sound counts, he said, the least sound and the least syllable. His illustration of this observation was wholly characteristic: he told of how he had wakened that week after midnight and heard the sounds made by a cat walking delicately and carefully on the crusted snow outside his house. He was listening, as in his lifelong vigil of awareness, for such phrases as this one, describing autumn leaves: "The skreak and skritter of evening gone." No single one of thousands of such inventions is enough to suggest his genius for experience and language.

After his comment, Stevens returned to his typescript, prepared and bound for the occasion with a fabulous elegance which also was characteristic: but an old Cambridge lady, holding an ear trumpet aloft, and dressed in a style which must have been chic at Rutherford Hayes' inauguration, shouted out, hoarse and peremptory as crows, that she must ask Mr. Stevens to speak loudly and clearly, loudly and clearly, if you please. She might just as well have been shouting at President Hayes. Stevens continued in a very low voice, reading poems which were written in that bravura style, that extravagant, luxurious, misunderstood rhetoric which is as passionate as the most excited Elizabethan blank verse. And throughout the reading, although Stevens was extremely nervous and constrained, this showed only as a rigid impossibility which, since it might have expressed a very different state of mind, made his feelings invisible; nevertheless, as such readings became more frequent in recent years, it was impossible to persuade Stevens that no one save himself perceived his overwhelming nervousness, just as, when the first reading ended, Stevens said to the teacher who had introduced him: "I wonder what the boys at the office would think of this?" The office was the Hartford Accident and Indemnity Co., the boys were those who knew him as a vice-president, lawyer, and the most solid of citizens.

No one who thought a poet looked pale, distracted, unkempt and unbarbered was likely to recognize Stevens: he was a physical giant, robust, red-faced, and his large round head suggested not only a banker and judge, but Jupiter. He said then and after that the boys would hardly be more shocked to discover him the secret head of an opium ring — and although I would guess that in this instance he may have mistaken tact for ignorance — the important point is that he felt sure that this was how others regarded a poet. He had written poetry for many years as a kind of "secret vice," and he told many stories about himself of the same kind, resorting to that self-irony which often marks his poetic style.

It was this sense of what it was to be a poet in America which haunted Stevens and inspired his poems; yet if this sense was rooted in American life during his first youth in the 1890s and 1900s, Stevens also belonged to the great and tragic generation, in Europe, of Proust, Valéry, and Kafka; for he was only four years younger than Rilke and three years older than Joyce whom he most resembled as a master and revolutionist of language. This temporal and spiritual kinship is often overlooked, probably because his first book did not appear until he was 44, and then the critical comments disheartened him so much that he stopped writing for several years, so that his second book did not appear until he was 57. His intimate relationship with his own generation in Europe did not diminish but rather intensified the way in which he was a purely American poet.

*　　*
*

It is clearly too soon to estimate the value of Stevens' poetry with justice, and nothing short of a detailed essay would make plausible what will surely seem personal and an over-estimation, my own conviction that the more than 500 pages of Stevens' *Collected Poems* make a book as important as *Leaves of Grass*. The very charm and beauty of Stevens' language misleads the reader often: delighted with the tick and tock, the high ho of Hoon and Jocundus, "jubilating," "in the presto of the morning," the reader often missed the basic substance, the joy that for the moment at least the poet has grasped "the veritable *ding an sich* at last": for Stevens was essentially a philosophical poet, the rarest of all kinds, seeking always "in a good light for those who know the ultimate Plato," to see and possess "the nothing that is not there, and the nothing that is." It is natural enough not to recognize that a poem called "Le Monocle de Mon Oncle" is a serous discourse on the nature of love; a poem named "The Comedian As the Letter C," may be a serious analysis of the perennial attitudes toward experience, but it is much longer than most poems that most readers of poetry read; and the title of "Thirteen Ways of Looking At a Blackbird" hardly makes clear the fact that its subject is everything involved in looking, loving, and living.

*   *
*

How, reading such [poems], which are a multitude, can we fail to understand the poet's triumphant affirmation: "What more is there to love than I have loved?" and lived? The Hoon — the human alone — which he calls himself in a number of poems became in his recent work Jocundus; his poems became "The auroras of Autumn"; Peter Quince "at the clavier" became "Professor Eucalyptus," declaring that "the search for reality is as momentous as the search for god," making continual "addresses to the Academy of Fine Ideas," and once more reporting, in the last poem of his collected volume, on "the thing itself"; a bird's "scrawny cry," in the first morning, is that of "a chorister whose c preceded the choir," it is a part of "the colossal sun's choral rings" and it is truly "a new knowledge of reality": Prince of the realm and of English, majestic voice, sovereign of the mind and of light, master of reality.

Richard Wright
1908–1960

by

JAMES BALDWIN

UNLESS A WRITER is extremely old when he dies, in which case he has probably become a neglected institution, his death must always seem untimely. This is because a real writer is always shifting and changing and searching. The world has many labels for him, of which the most treacherous is the label of Success. But the man behind the label knows defeat far more intimately than he knows triumph. He can never be absolutely certain that he has achieved his intention.

This tension and authority — the authority of the frequently defeated — are in the writer's work, and cause one to feel that, at the moment of his death, he was approaching his greatest achievements. I should think that guilt plays some part in this reaction, as well as a certain unadmitted relief. Guilt, because of our failure in a relationship, because it is extremely difficult to deal with writers as people. Writers are said to be extremely egotistical and demanding and they are indeed, but that does not distinguish them from anyone else. What distinguishes them is what James once described as a kind of "holy stupidity." The writer's greed is appalling. He wants, or seems to want, everything and practically everybody; in another sense, and at the same time, he needs no one at all; and families, friends, and lovers find this extremely hard to take. While he is alive, his work is fatally entangled with his personal fortunes and misfortunes, his personality, and the social facts and attitudes of his time. The unadmitted relief, then, of which I spoke has to do with a certain drop in the intensity of our bewilderment, for the baffling creator no longer stands between us and his works.

He does not, but many things do, above all our own pre-occupations. In the case of Richard Wright, dead in Paris at fifty-two, the fact that he worked during a bewildering and demoralizing era in Western history makes a proper assessment of his work more difficult. In *Eight Men,* the earliest story, "The Man Who Saw the Flood," takes place in the Deep South and was first published in 1937. One of the two previously unpublished stories in the book, "Man, God Ain't Like That," begins in Africa, achieves its hideous resolution in Paris, and brings us, with an ironical and fitting grimness, to the threshold of the 1960s. It is because of this story, which is remarkable, and "Man of All Work," which is a masterpiece, that I cannot avoid feeling that Wright, as he died, was acquiring a new tone, and a less uncertain esthetic distance, and a new depth.

Shortly after we learned of Richard Wright's death, a Negro woman who was rereading *Native Son* told me that it meant more to her now than it had when she had first read it. This, she said, was because the specific social climate which had produced it, or with which it was identified, seemed archaic now, was fading from our memories. Now, there was only the book itself to deal with, for it could no longer be read, as it had been read in 1940, as a militant racial manifesto. Today's racial manifestoes were being written very differently, and in many different languages; what mattered about the book now was how accurately or deeply the life of Chicago's South Side had been conveyed.

*   *
*

It is strange to begin to suspect, now, that Richard Wright was never really the social and polemical writer he took himself to be. In my own relations with him, I was always exasperated by his notions of society, politics, and history, for he seemed to me utterly fanciful. I never believed that he had any real sense of how a society is put together. It had not occurred to me, and perhaps it had not occurred to him, that his major interest as well as his power lay elsewhere. Or perhaps it had occurred to me, for I distrusted his association with the French intellectuals, Sartre, de Beauvoir, and company. I am not being vindictive toward them or condescending toward Richard Wright when I say that it seemed to me that there was very little they could give him which he could use. It has always seemed to me that ideas were somewhat more real to them than people; but anyway, and this is a statement made with the very greatest love and respect, I always sensed in Richard Wright a Mississippi pickaninny, mischievous, cunning, and tough. This always seemed to be at the bottom of everything he said and did, like some fantastic jewel buried in high grass. And it was painful to feel that the people of his adopted country were no more capable of seeing this jewel than were the people of this native land, and were in their own way as intimidated by it.

Even more painful was the suspicion that Wright did not want to know this. The meaning of Europe for an

American Negro was one of the things about which Richard Wright and I disagreed most vehemently. He was fond of referring to Paris as the "city of refuge" — which it certainly was, God knows, for the likes of us. But it was not a city of refuge for the French, still less for anyone belonging to France; and it would not have been a city of refuge for us if we had not been armed with American passports. It did not seem worthwhile to me to have fled the native fantasy only to embrace a foreign one. (Someone, some day, should do a study in depth of the role of the American Negro in the mind and life of Europe, and the extraordinary peril, different from those of America but not less grave, which the American Negro encounters in the Old World.)

* * *

I was far from imagining, when I agreed to write this memoir, that it would prove to be such a painful and difficult task. What, after all, can I really say about Richard...? Everything founders in the sea of what might have been. We might have been friends, for example, but I cannot honestly say that we were. There might have been some way of avoiding our quarrel, our rupture; I can only say that I failed to find it. The quarrel having occurred, perhaps there might have been a way to have become reconciled. I think, in fact, that I counted on this coming about in some mysterious, irrevocable way, the way a child dreams of winning, by means of some dazzling exploit, the love of his parents.

However, he is dead now, and so we never shall be reconciled. The debt I owe him can now never be discharged, at least not in the way I hoped to be able to discharge it. In fact, the saddest thing about our relationship is that my only means of discharging my debt to Richard was to become a writer; and this effort revealed, more and more clearly as the years went on, the deep and irreconcilable differences between our points of view.

This might not have been so serious if I had been older when we met. . . . If I had been, that is, less uncertain of my-self, and less monstrously egotistical. But when we met, I was twenty, a carnivorous age; he was then as old as I am now, thirty-six; he had been my idol since high school, and I, as the fledgling Negro writer, was very shortly in the position of his protégé. This position was not really fair to either of us. As writers we were about as unlike as any two writers could possibly be. But no one can read the future, and neither of us knew this then. We were linked together, really, because both of us were black. I had made my pil-grimage to meet him because he was the greatest black writer in the world for me. In *Uncle Tom's Children*, in *Native Son*, and, above all, in *Black Boy*, I found expressed, for the first time in my life, the sorrow, the rage, and the murder-ous bitterness which was eating up my life and the lives of those around me. His work was an immense liberation and revelation for me. He became my ally and my witness, and alas! my father.

*   *   *

Well, he worked up until the end, died, as I hope to do, in the middle of a sentence, and his work is now an irre-ducible part of the history of our swift and terrible time. Whoever He may be, and wherever you may be, may God be with you, Richard, and may He help me not to fail that argument which you began in me.

Ernest Hemingway
1899–1961

by

ARCHIBALD MACLEISH

I WROTE A POEM some years ago in which there was a question about Hemingway and an answer:

> *. . . The lad in the Rue de Notre Dame des Champs*
> *In the carpenter's loft on the left-hand side going down —*
> *The lad with the supple look like a sleepy panther —*
> *And what became of him? Fame became of him.*
> *Veteran out of the wars before he was twenty.*
> *Famous at twenty-five: thirty a master —*
> *Whittled a style for his time from a walnut stick*
> *In a carpenter's loft in a street of that April city.*

Now, with his death, the question asks itself again: what became of him?

How shall that question be answered now? By the fame still? I don't suppose any writer since Byron has been as famous as Hemingway was when he died, but fame is a young man's passion. It has little to say to the fact of death.

Or is the style the answer? The style remains as surely as the fame. It has been praised, imitated and derided for

30 years, but it endures: the one intrinsic style our century has produced. And yet Hemingway was the last man to wish to be remembered as a stylist, and none of his critics, however much he has admired the style or detested it, has been able or willing to leave his judgment at that.

To answer one must go further back. It is not Hemingway's death or even the manner of his death which poses the question now; it is his life — the fact that his life is over and demands to be looked at, to be measured. What makes the answer difficult is that Hemingway's life was a strange life for a writer, as we think of writers in our time. Writers with us are supposed to be watchers. "God's spies" as John Keats put it once. They are supposed to spend themselves observing the world, watching history and mankind and themselves — particularly themselves: their unsaid thoughts, their secret deeds and dreads. Hemingway was not a watcher: he was an actor in his life. He took part. What he took part in was not the private history of Ernest Hemingway or the social history of Oak Park, Illinois, or the intellectual history of a generation of his fellow countrymen. What he took part in was a public — even a universal — history of wars and animals and gigantic fish. And he did take part. He could never go to a war — and he went to every war available to him — without engaging in it. He went to the First World War as an ambulance driver and got his knee smashed by a shell in a front-line trench where no one had sent him. He went to the war in Spain to write a scenario for a movie and learned how you washed the powder burns off your hands without water. He went to the last World War as a correspondent — and worried the high command by turning up with other tools than typewriters — mementos he called them. And between wars there were lions and elephants. And between elephants and lions there were marlin. Also bears.

*   *
*

A strange life for a writer and a difficult life to judge at the end. Indeed, a difficult life to judge before the end — which is perhaps why Hemingway attracted, alive, more critics of more schools and opinions than most writers who have been dead for centuries. Writers generally are judged by their work, but Hemingway's life kept threatening to get in the way of his work with the result that his critics never found themselves in agreement. Those who were drawn to him called him, as one of them actually did on the day of his death, "a man who lived it up to write it down." Those who were repelled — and most of the hostile critics seemed to have been repelled emotionally as well as intellectually — called him in one form of words or another a phony: a man who ran away from his real task to masquerade as a big game hunter or a hero or a tough guy. What they will say now I don't know — perhaps that he had run as fast as he could and that the truth caught up with him at 7:30 on the morning of the second of July.

Both views are based on a misconception of the relation between a writer's task and a writer's life. Both conceive of life and writing as different and even contradictory things. The deploring critic thinks of Hemingway's life as a betrayal of his obligation: you don't fight marlin by the hour and watch the killing of 1,500 bulls if you are loyal to your writer's obligation to your craft. The admiring critic thinks of the obligation as incidental to the life: you shoot grizzlies and then you write about it. Or that understanding the simple and primary fact that writing — true writing — is not the natural by-product of an isolated experience, not the autonomous creation of an isolated man, but the consequence of a collision between the two. Neither realizes that the collision when it occurs, even when the experience is a lion in the gun sights or a German in a Normandy hedge, may provide, for the right writer, something more than a thrill and something very different from an escape. It may, indeed, provide realization — precisely such a realization as the art of letters at the greatest is capable of providing, the realization of the meaning of a man. Danger is not the least revealing of the mirrors into which we look.

That this obvious fact was obvious to Hemingway is a matter of record. Long before he had money enough for a safari or time enough to compose a theory of esthetics, had he ever wished to compose one, he had learned that lesson. Of the time in his 20s when he was learning to write, he said, "I found the greatest difficulty aside from knowing truly what you really felt, rather than what you were supposed to feel ... was to put down what really happened in action: what the actual things were which produced the emotion that you experienced." The problem, that is to say, was to master the collision of man and event, writer and experience in both its terms: the perception of the event as it really was and the recognition of the emotion that the event really exerted. A later remark of his added another dimension to the task. In a letter to a young man who had sent him some imitative work he said: "... See the things you write about not through my eyes and my ears but through your own with your language." To see "with language," to see "what really happened in action" and to recognize "what you really felt, rather than what you were supposed to feel" with language was a writer's task as Hemingway saw it. Most writers I think would agree that the task was well seen and that accomplishment of the task so defined would be anything but a betrayal of the obligation which every writer assumes. To put together what "really" happened and what you "really" felt as you faced it is not only to see the lion but to understand the man. The writer who can do this, as Hemingway demonstrated that he could, is no less a poet of the human experience — God's spy — than the writer who spied upon nearer and more familiar worlds.

*   *
*

What became of Hemingway? Fame became of him, yes, but something more, I think, than fame. Art became of him — became of him in the truest and the largest sense. Rilke once said of the writing of a verse: it is not enough merely to feel; one must also see and touch and know. But it is not enough, either, to see and touch and know: one must have memories of love and pain and death. But not even these memories are enough: the memories must be "turned to blood within us" so that they are no longer distinguishable from ourselves. Experience, Rilke was declaring, must turn into man before a poem can be written. Experience, that is to say, must reach such an intensity that it contains our own being. When that happens — when experience and man *so* meet — the poem may be written and when the poem is written we may discover who we are.

Hemingway brought himself to face experience of this intensity not once, but more than once. And what became of him was that great triumph.

James Thurber
1894–1961

by

E. B. WHITE

I AM ONE of the lucky ones. I knew him before blindness hit him, before fame hit him, and I tend always to think of him as a young artist in a small office in a big city, with all the world still ahead. It was a fine thing to be young and at work in New York, for a new magazine when Thurber was young and at work, and I will always be glad that this happened to me.

It was fortunate that we got on well, the office we shared was the size of a hall bedroom. There was just room enough for two men, two typewriters, and a stack of copy paper. The copy paper disappeared at a scandalous rate — not because our production was high (although it was) but because Thurber used copy paper as the natural receptacle for discarded sorrows, immediate joys, stale dreams, golden prophecies, and messages of good cheer to the outside world and to fellow-workers. His mind was never at rest, and his pencil was connected to his mind by the best conductive tissue I have ever seen in action. The whole world knows what a funny man he was, but you had to sit next to him day after day to understand the extravagance of his clowning, the wildness and subtlety of his thinking, and the intensity of his interest in others and his sympathy for their dilemmas — dilemmas that he instantly enlarged, put in focus, and made immortal, just as he enlarged and made immortal the strange goings on in the Ohio home of his boyhood. His waking dreams and his sleeping dreams commingled shamelessly and uproariously. Ohio was never far from his thoughts, and when he received a medal from his home state in 1953, he wrote, "The clocks that strike in my dreams are often the clocks of Columbus." It is a beautiful sentence and a revealing one.

He was both a practitioner of humor and a defender of it. The day he died, I came on a letter from him, dictated to a secretary and signed in pencil with his sightless and enormous "Jim." "Every time is a time for humor," he wrote. "I write humor the way a surgeon operates, because it is a livelihood, because I have a great urge to do it, because many interesting challenges are set up, and because I have the hope it may do some good." Once, I remember, he heard someone say that humor is a shield, not a sword, and it made him mad. He wasn't going to have anyone beating his sword into a shield. That "surgeon," incidentally, is pure Mitty. During his happiest years, Thurber did not write the way a surgeon operates, he wrote the way a child skips rope, the way a mouse waltzes.

Although he is best known for *Walter Mitty* and *The Male Animal*, the book of his I like best is *The Last Flower*. In it you will find his faith in the renewal of life, his feeling for the beauty and fragility of life on earth. Like all good writers, he fashioned his own best obituary notice. Nobody else can add to the record, much as he might like to. And if all the flowers, real and figurative, that will find their way to Thurber's last resting place, the one that will remain fresh and wiltproof is the little flower he himself drew, on the last page of that lovely book.

an indignant rage because she had been turned out of her college when it was discovered that she had married him secretly. She thought the attitude of the college to her marriage was hysterical and absurd, as though the fact of being married had made her an initiate into something too dark and dangerous for the others to be near. It was a witness to what she protested against in "Spinster".

* * *

After Sylvia graduated they went to America, and taught and wrote and began to publish more poems. When they came back to England they lived in London for a while and I saw them once in their flat there. It was off Regent's Park, the top floor of a house which had been caught on the edge of collapse and nursed back to charm and usefulness by some enterprising person who was now spreading his restorations further. It was in 1960 when Sylvia had just had her first baby, Frieda. Their flat was painted white and excitingly filled with objects, and photographic blow-ups that made me long to stay and examine it minutely. But I had only time to rush in and out. Some months later they came to Cambridge for a day and a night, bringing Frieda and a friend of theirs who had been staying with them. I was interested to see the calm affectionate pleasure with which Sylvia dealt with Frieda. Once more the lack of fuss, the efficiency, the collectedness.

* * *

This was the last time I saw them. They moved to Devon after that and seemed to be very busy and absorbed in their lives and their writing. When, two years later, I heard that

Sylvia had killed herself I was simply unable to believe it. Suicide often seems to be a very reasonable means of leaving a disastrous life but it was very difficult to connect Sylvia with self-slaughter. Her attitude to life was, as I had seen it, so wholly and sensitively positive, that I had at first a ludicrous conviction that she must have been murdered. Then I read *The Bell Jar* and *Ariel*, and it became clearer to me how it had come about. Nevertheless for me, Sylvia's quality, her personal style of being, her vitality are summed up in an image of the Winged Victory as I have seen it flood-lit in the Louvre. She strides, her robes fly out, beautiful and huge. The disaster that befell Sylvia from within was a final version of the same disaster that is on a lesser scale recurrent for most of us. An eclipse of the light, temporary but recurring. She succumbed, in a dark phase of the moon, to the serpent that had followed her all her life.

Sylvia was serious and truthful and highly evolved — Forsterian terms; she was wholly remarkable for being wholly authentic. By which I mean that she was true to herself, or truly herself, something which is exceedingly rare. She was incapable of any sort of falsity or affectation or exaggeration. Her desire was to catch her life at its widest and richest stretch and live it with comprehension. But along with her remarkable abilities (in which she took no possessive pride since she took them for granted as the given), she had a streak of sharp contempt for anyone who appeared to refuse the full range of human experience. (She had no patience with compromises and smallness. To excel, she took for granted: that was merely the starting point: it was the thing itself that mattered to her.) She also had a bitter grief and resentment at the pain involved in being human, for herself and (by identification) for the rest of humanity. She could neither tolerate the pain herself, nor bear it for anyone else. It seems that an acceptance of the fact of pain is necessary for survival. The digestion of that excruciating fact is the price of survival. She explored everything that happened to her with precision and courage, and in time she would have arrived at that exciting point where tolerance fertilizes experience with compassion. If she had lived she would have paid that price.

Robert Frost
1874–1963

by

JOHN CIARDI

A FEW YEARS AGO practically everyone at the Bread
Loaf Writers' Conference drove the four miles or so down-
mountain to the tiny town of Ripton for the showing of a
United States Information Service film about Robert Frost,
the proceeds of the showing to go into a new paint job for
the community center. There, in the name of good causes,
we sat while some fool's dream of gorgeous-gorgeous Tech-
nicolor and trick camera angles made Vermont into garish
postcards. And through that country that never was, there
wandered the lonely but benign figure of an old man
named Robert Frost, doddering from here to there at the
prompting of a director who must have learned his trade
in a marzipan factory.

So ran our government's image-for-export of America's best artist. The night after this cloying performance,
Robert Frost asked me what I had thought of it and I had
to confess that I had not liked it.

"Why?" he said, with a kind of brusque mock-fierceness
that those who knew him could take for a sign that he was
interested in the subject.

"Because," I said, groping for a moment and then finding the way to say it, "Robert Frost is no lollipop."

Someone came along at that point and the talk headed off on another tack. I had all but forgotten our brief exchange when, the next year at Bread Loaf and in another context, Mr. Frost said to me, "It's as you said once. I'm no lollipop."

I have never known a man who was less one. Robert Frost was a primal energy. There were serenities in the man as time brought them to him, but there was in him a volcano of passion that burned to his last day. Many of his readers, alas, have drawn back from that earth-passion in him. Incapable of living at such heat, they have moved away and pretended to admire him from a cool distance as part of a picturesque landscape. Let me yet hope that no man, for sentimental reasons, will be moved to eulogize the confectionary image of a kindly, vague, white-haired great-grandfather when there is the reality of a magnificently passionate man to honor.

No man makes it into the dimensions of a Robert Frost on simple sweetness. There is not that much combustion in sugar. To be greatly of the earth demands the bitter sweat and scald of first passions. That heat could erupt into cantankerousness at times, and even into the occasional meanness of which violent temper is capable. But the splutters of cantankerousness and the violences of temper were only surface bubbles on the magmatic passions of the man, part of the least traits that accompany intensity.

It is just that passionate intensity that must be realized before the man can by loved, mourned — and read — in his own nature. And what better mourns a poet than the act of reading him again, so to be stored and restored by him? But take him for sugar, and the world is mush, its homage a sickly mockery.

It is, perhaps, one of the saddest marks of our times that the best of our artists, once they have lost the first strangeness of what is wild in all true creation, once they have lived out their achievement in general acceptance, can so readily be taken as figures of tame sentiment. Let the memory of a great man be spared such nonsense. His genius, wild and ardent, remains to us in his poems. It is the man we lose, a man salty and rough with the earth trace, and though towering above it, never removed from it, a man above all who could tower precisely because he was rooted in real earth. It is the earth-grip that lets a man stand tallest.

He was our best. And certainly to honor him in the truth of himself is a least homage. Yet the sentimental distortion remains fixed in the public mind, and has marred every public recognition tendered him from honorable sentiment but in the blindness of sentimentality. When, at a dinner given in honor of Mr. Frost's eighty-fifth birthday, Lionel Trilling praised him as a terrifying and Sophoclean poet, a central quality of Mr. Frost's character and genius was nobly identified and justly honored. Yet even so high an appraisal became the occasion for outraged journalism, and for no reason I could see but that the word "terrifying" suggests a reality rather than a sentimental evasion. What but terror — the terror of a passionately engaged tragic life-sense — informs so Frostian a poem as "Fire and Ice"? Or such a poem as "To Earthward"? Let the concluding lines of "To Earthward" speak the man as the true readers of poetry will know him to all time:

Now no joy but lacks salt
That is not dashed with pain
And weariness and fault;
I crave the stain

Of tears, the aftermark
Of almost too much love,
The sweet of bitter bark
And burning clove.

When stiff and sore and scarred
I take away my hand
From leaning on it hard
In grass and sand,

The hurt is not enough:
I long for weight and strength
To feel the earth as rough
To all my length.

May there be briary souls, real beasts, and the heat and cold and stain of the earth in the place to which such men go. And if there is no such place in fact, the better reason to build its image within the memory we keep of those who lived their great lives in the power of such passions as may fill our lesser ones with the rankness of reality at the roots, and only then stretch them toward the liberating sky-reach.

by

HUGH KENNER

H<small>IS INNOCENCE LINGERS</small>: innocence and aching vulnerability. He went unprotected by any public role. He wouldn't have known how to be a literary man if he had wanted to try. One day he read from his poems, for an hour or so, in (wasn't it?) a Newark department store, more or less heard, one imagines by holiday shoppers. He would have been seventy-five then, and he did it because he was invited to. (Who could have invited him? The management?) He believed fiercely in poems, in a public need for words released, set dancing: he would do anything at all to serve that belief.

> *. . . Look at*
>   *what passes for the new*
>   *You will not find it there but in*
>   *despised poems.*
>   *It is difficult*
>   *to get the news from poems*
>   *yet men die miserably every day*
>   *for lack*
>   *of what is found there. . . .*

Yet so disengaged was he from his own achievement that he died, six months short of his eightieth birthday, pathetically unpersuaded of its magnitude. It was the only pathetic trait in an indomitable man.

For no role sustained him. Has any poet ever before rejected so radically the stay, and temptation, of poet's status? It was a heroic venture, persisted in for six decades. Williams struck a miraculous equilibrium; he did a job as a poet, and with such passion and tenacity that American poetry groups itself around twin peaks, Williams and Whitman; but as to what he was, he was a physician. The careers twinned from the start.

He had the physician's toughness, the physician's irritability. He had had his sleep broken too often by nuisance house-calls to cosset his medical life in sentimentalities. All those people whom he served with passion upheld him and encroached on him. He had stood by too often at needless deaths to believe in either the infallible power of man to intervene, or in the capacity of merely conventional words to sustain. The bereaved long for words, the dying long to speak them. It is when we try to speak from the heart that we understand how man's way is smoothed by ritual, and regret the deadness of our residual rituals in a pragmatic time.

The pathetic verse whose neck Williams saw no point in wringing, the limp iambic rhymes that struggled up toward heaven in 1910 out of every opened magazine in New Jersey, constituted a dead residual ritual, pointless, offensive. He set out to carry American verse in one lifetime, by sheer intensity of application, all the way from demotic speech to indigenous ceremony: "a reply to Greek and Latin with the bare hands."

Every day in his consulting room people struggled and stammered, the illiterate people as well as the normally glib, to convey the simplest matters, matters justifying an often difficult journey to an interview that would have to be paid for: my child's pallor, my aching foot, and the meaning of these facts in worry and disequilibrium.

No poet has had a better chance to know how people are lost when they set about examining their lives, or to listen to American speech rhythms under stress. He wanted speech to issue as though unpremeditated, word after word to drop into place: the bare truth to sing.

> *Let the snake wait under*
> *his weed*
> *and the writing*
> *be of words, slow and quick, sharp*
> *to strike, quiet to wait,*
> *sleepless.*
> *— through metaphor to reconcile*
> *the people and the stones.*
> *Compose. (No ideas*
> *but in things) Invent!*
> *Saxifrage is my flower that splits*
> *the rocks.*

As the professional golfer can count on sinking a ten-foot putt at one stroke, so years of tireless practice permitted him, sometimes, to write in fifteen minutes a poem as durable as the language can conceive. Those were the quarter-hours he lived for. In old age, crippled by stroke after stroke, his speech impaired, his right hand paralyzed, he would still sit early of a morning at his electric type-writer, dropping the maneuvered finger on one key after another, writing and rewriting sometimes brief sketches, sometimes very long poems. The fifth part of *Paterson*, the great meditation on love and on his own death ("Asphodel, that Greeny Flower"), the whole of the work contained in *Pictures from Breughel*, came out of those years.

Language and the Poet

A lifetime's discipline raised up, out of the pain and plodding and confusion of those last mornings, an effortless artless eloquence, as tender or as vigorous as he could want it to be: as though he had been schooling himself all his life for the time when he would have his freest work to do, and would have to do it under those conditions. The first four books of *Paterson* (1946-51) are his most solid achievement; the last work (*Pictures from Breughel*, 1962) the most poignant, simplest and loveliest. He has brought the language by concern and love to an utter, feminine responsiveness. He wrote often about the language itself, and about the imagination's way with it: never better than in the "Song" he conceived one morning with Botticelli's Venus somewhere in his limpid, eager mind, and saw printed in this magazine two years ago:

> beauty is a shell
> from the sea
> where she rules triumphant
> till love has had its way with her
> scallops and
> lion's paws

Sculptured to the
tune of retreating waves
undying accents
repeated till
the ear and the eye lie
down together in the same bed

Flannery O'Connor
1925–1964

by

KATHERINE ANNE PORTER

I SAW OUR lovely and gifted Flannery O'Connor only three times over a period, I think, of three years or more, but each meeting was spontaneously an occasion and I want to write about her just as she impressed me.

I want to tell what she looked like and how she carried herself and how she sounded standing balanced lightly on her aluminum crutches, whistling to her peacocks who came floating and rustling to her, calling in their rusty voices.

I do not want to speak of her work because we all know what it was and we don't need to say what we think about it but to read and understand what she was trying to tell us.

Now and again there hovers on the margin of the future a presence that one feels as imminent — if I may use stylish vocabulary. She came up among us like a presence, a carrier of a gift not to be disputed but welcomed. She lived among us like a presence and went away early, leaving her harvest perhaps not yet all together gathered, though, like so many geniuses who have small time in this world. I think she had her warning and accepted it and did her work even if we all would like to have had her stay on forever and do more.

It is all very well for those who are left to console themselves. She said what she had to say. I'm pretty certain that her work was finished. We shouldn't mourn for her but for ourselves and our loves.

After all, I saw her just twice — memory has counted it three — for the second time was a day-long affair at a conference and a party given by Flannery's mother in the evening. And I want to tell you something I think is amusing because Flannery lived in such an old-fashioned Southern village very celebrated in Southern history on account of what took place during the War. But in the lovely, old, aerie, tall country home and the life of a young girl living with her mother in a country town so that there was almost no way for her knowing the difficulties of human beings and her general knowledge of this was really impressive because she was so very young and you wondered where — how — she had learned all that. But this is a question that everybody always asks himself about genius. I want to just tell something to illustrate the Southern custom.

Ladies in Society there — in that particular society, I mean — were nearly always known, no matter if they were married once or twice, they were known to their dying day by their maiden names. They were called "Miss Mary" or whatever it was. And so, Flannery's mother, too; her maiden name was Regina Cline and so she was still known as "Miss Regina Cline" and one evening at a party when I was there after the conference, someone mentioned Flannery's name and another — a neighbor, mind you, who had probably been around there all her life — said, "Who is Flannery O'Connor? I keep hearing about her." The other one said, "Oh you know! Why, that's Regina Cline's daughter: that little girl who writes." And that was the atmosphere in which her genius developed and her life was lived and her work was done. I myself think it a very healthy, good atmosphere because nobody got in her way, nobody tried to interfere with her or direct her and she lived easily and simply and in her own atmosphere and her own way of thinking. I believe this is the best possible way for a genius to live. I think that they're too often tortured by this world and when people discover that someone has a gift, they all come with their claws out, trying to snatch something of it, trying to share something they have no right even to touch. And she was safe from that: she had a mother who really took care of her. And I just think that's something we ought to mention, ought to speak of.

She managed to mix, somehow, two very different kinds of chickens and produced a bird hitherto unseen in this world. I asked her if she were going to send it to the County Fair. "I might, but first I must find a name for it. You name it!" she said. I thought of it many times but no fitting name for that creature ever occurred to me. And no fitting word now occurs to me to describe her stories, her particular style, her view of life, but I know its greatness and I see it — and see that it was one of the great gifts of our times.

I want to speak a little of her religious life though it was very sacred and quiet. She was as reserved about it as any saint. When I first met her, she and her mother were about to go on a seventeen-day trip to Lourdes. I said, "Oh, I wish I could go with you!" She said, "I wish you could. But I'll write you a letter." She never wrote that letter. She just sent a post card and she wrote: "The sight of faith and affliction joined in prayer — very impressive." That was all.

In some newspaper notice of her death, mention of her

self-portrait with her favorite peacock was made. It spoke of her plain features. She had unusual features but they were anything but plain. I saw that portrait in her home and she had not flattered herself. The portrait does have her features, in a way, but here's something else. She had a young softness and gentleness of face and expression. The look — something in the depth of the eyes and the fixed mouth; the whole pose fiercely intent gives an uncompromising glimpse of her character. Something you might not see on first or even second glance in that tenderly fresh-colored, young, smiling face; something she saw in herself, knew about herself, that she was trying to tell us in a way less personal, yet more vivid than words.

That portrait, I'm trying to say, looked like the girl who wrote those blood-curdling stories about human evil — NOT the living Flannery, whistling to her peacocks, showing off her delightfully freakish breed of chickens.

I want to thank you for giving me the opportunity to tell you about the Flannery O'Connor I know. I loved and valued her dearly, her work and her strange unworldly radiance of spirit in a human being so intelligent and un-deceived by the appearance of things. I would feel too badly if I did not honor myself by saying a word in her honor: it is a great loss.

T. S. Eliot
1888–1965

by

ALLEN TATE

A FEW DAYS after January 4th of last year I knew that I needed to do something about the loss I was becoming more and more aware of in the death of T. S. Eliot. On the afternoon of the 4th a reporter at *The New York Times* had telephoned me in Minneapolis and asked me for an "estimate of Mr. Eliot's place in modern literature" — and had I known him and could I think of any interesting anecdotes." This crass incident delayed the shock of realization; and it was several days later that I understood that T. S. Eliot was dead. One dies every day one's own death, but one cannot imagine the death of the man who was *il maestro di color che sanno* — or, since he was an artist and not, after his young manhood, a philosopher: *il maestro di color che scrivono.* To see his maestro, Dante had to "lift his eyelids a little higher," and that was what I knew, after January 4th, I had been doing in the thirty-six years of an acquaintance that almost imperceptibly became friendship. I looked up to him, and in doing so I could not feel myself in any sense diminished. What he thought of "us" — by us, I mean his old but slightly younger literary friends — we never quite knew because he never quite said. The un-Eliot or anti-

Eliot people thought that his literary reticence was "cagey" and ungenerous. It was the highest form of civility. If he didn't know whether we were good writers it was because he didn't know, in spite of his immense fame, whether he himself would last. Somewhere, in print, he put himself with Yeats. But would Yeats last? I am sure he didn't know. He was simply aware — and he would have been obtuse had he not been aware — that he and Yeats dominated poetry in English in this century; but that, to a deeply empirical mind, meant little in the long run of posterity.

What then could I do? On the death of a friend one may meditate the Thankless Muse, even if the friend was not a poet. The meditation becomes more difficult, and one almost gives it up, if the friend is not only a poet but perhaps a great poet. The poet-as-Greatness is not, as our friend might have said in his Harvard dissertation on F. H. Bradley, an object of knowledge: it is only a point of view. Private meditation at best must land one in the midst of The Last Things, beyond the common reality; but poetry begins with the common reality, and ends with it, as our friend's friend, Charles Williams, said of Dante. It could be equally said of Tom Eliot; and that is why it is not inappropriate, on this occasion, to see him first as a man, and to speak plainly of him as Tom; for he was the uncommon man committed to the common reality of the human condition. Only men so committed, and so deeply committed that there is no one moment in their lives when they are aware of an act of commitment, express the perfect simplicity of manners that was Tom Eliot's. . . .

What — I repeat the question — what, then, could I do? What could I do about the loss I felt in the death not of Tom Eliot but of T. S. Eliot? I almost distinguish the two persons because my friendship with Tom Eliot was a private matter to which the public might have indirect access only if I were capable of writing a formal pastoral elegy like "Lycidas"; but then Tom Eliot would become T. S. Eliot the public figure, a figure considerably larger than his elegist. Is it not customary for the greater man to appropriate the elegiac mode to celebrate the hitherto unknown talents of the lesser? Had Milton's friend King been a great poet Milton could not have *somewhat* loudly swept the strings: he might have been tempted to indulge in hyperbole instead of what he did, which was to forget King, as posterity was to forget him, and give us Milton. Whatever I might do about Tom Eliot or T. S. Eliot, I could not forget him and exhibit the dubious poetic virtuosity of Tate.

What I could do is what I have done, for what one does reveals the limit of what one can do. I have brought together, at the invitation of the editor of *The Sewanee Review*, some twenty essays in reminiscence and appreciation. But there is no invasion of the severe privacy which Tom Eliot the man and T. S. Eliot the poet maintained throughout his seventy-six years. His poems came out of the fiery crucible of his interior life; yet all of the interior life that we know is in the poems; and that is as it should be: for his theory of the impersonality of poetry met no contradiction in the intensely personal origins of the poems. When I asked his old friends to write essays I hoped that they would bear witness to the part that his character and mind had played in their lives and works.

*　　　*

*

This meditation has been difficult to write. I have not been consistent in my attempt to distinguish Tom Eliot from

T. S. Eliot; perhaps I should not have tried. As I look back upon the thirty-six years of our friendship I see that Tom gradually emerged from T. S., forming a double image of a unified mind and sensibility. I first met him in London in 1928, at one of the *Criterion* luncheons, to which Herbert Read had invited me and to which Frank Morley took me. There had been some formal correspondence as early as 1923 concerning some of my early poems which he had declined to publish in *The Criterion*. Years later, in 1956, when he was my guest in Minneapolis, I showed him his first letter to me in which he said that I ought to try to "simplify" myself — advice that I was never able to take, try as I would. When he had finished reading the letter, with that sober attention that he always gave to the most trivial request of a friend, looking over his spectacles, he said: "It seems awfully pompous and condescending"; and then he laughed. His laugh was never hearty; it was something between a chuckle and a giggle; and now he was laughing both at himself and at me — at me for what he evidently considered the absurdity of keeping a letter of his all those years.

In the autumn of 1958 I was at tea with him and his wife Valerie at their flat in Kensington Court Gardens. I arrived a little late and mumbling an apology said that I had had a late lunch with The Honorable. . . . He was a member of a millionaire American family that had migrated to England in the 1870s or '80s and had been ennobled. Tom (not T. S.) smiled and glanced at his wife. He said: "We had not heard of *them* before the War Between the States." I suppose I must explain this sectional joke. Tom Eliot, as everybody knows, was of New England origin, and would not have called that war the War Between the States had I not been present. He was telling his wife and me that he thought those people "newcomers" but he was slyly attributing the prejudice to me as a Southerner who might be supposed to take an unfavorable view of New York millionaires. I cannot think of a better example of the complex simplicity of his humor; and British as he became in many ways, his humor was unmistakably American.

by

ROBERT LOWELL

Wʜᴇɴ I ғɪʀsᴛ ᴍᴇᴛ Rᴀɴᴅᴀʟʟ, he was twenty-three
or -four, and unsettlingly brilliant, precocious, knowing,
naïve, and vexing. He seemed to make no distinction between what he would say in our hearing and what he would
say behind our backs. If anything, absence made him more
discreet. Woe to the acquaintance who liked the wrong
writer, the wrong poem by the right writer, or the wrong
lines in the right poem! And how those who loved him enjoyed admiring, complaining, and gossiping about the last
outrageous thing he had done or, more often, said. It
brought us together — whispering about Randall. In 1937,
we both roomed at the house of John Crowe Ransom in
Gambier, Ohio. Ransom and Jarrell had each separately
spent the preceding summer studying Shakespeare's sonnets, and had emerged with unorthodox and widely differ-
ing theories. Roughly, Ransom thought that Shakespeare
was continually going off the rails into illogical incoherence.
Jarrell believed that no one, not even William Empson, had
done justice to the rich, significant ambiguity of Shakespeare's intelligence and images. I can see and hear Ransom
and Jarrell now, seated on one sofa, as though on one love

[134]

seat, the sacred texts open on their laps, one fifty, the other just out of college, and each expounding to the other's deaf ears his own inspired and irreconcilable interpretation.

Gordon Chalmer, the president of Kenyon College, and a disciple of the somber anti-romantic humanists, once went skiing with Randall, and was shocked to hear him exclaiming, "I feel just like an angel." Randall *did* somehow give off an angelic impression, despite his love for tennis, singular mufflers knitted by a girlfriend, and disturbing improvements of his own on the latest dance steps. His mind, unearthly in its quickness, was a little boyish, disembodied, and brittle. His body was a little ghostly in its immunity to soil, entanglements, and rebellion. As one sat with him in oblivious absorption of the campus bar, sucking a fifteen-cent chocolate milkshake and talking eternal things, one felt, beside him, too corrupt and companionable. He had the harsh luminosity of Shelley — like Shelley, every inch a poet, and like Shelley, imperiled perhaps by an arid, abstracting precocity. Not really! Somewhere inside him, a breezy, untouchable spirit had even then made its youthful and sightless promise to accept — to accept and never to accept the bulk, confusion, and defeat of mortal flesh. . . . All that blithe and blood-torn dolor!

Randall Jarrell had his own peculiar and important excellence as a poet, and outdistanced all others in the things he could do well. His gifts, both by nature and by a lifetime of hard dedication and growth, were wit, pathos, and brilliance of intelligence. These qualities, dazzling in themselves, were often so well employed that he became, I think, the most heartbreaking English poet of his generation.

* *
*

He once said, "If I were a rich man, I would pay money for the privilege of being able to teach." Probably there was no better teacher of literature in the country, and yet he was curiously unworldly about it, and welcomed teaching for almost twenty years in the shade or heat of his little-known Southern college for girls in Greensboro, North Carolina. There his own community gave him a compact, tangible, personal reverence that was incomparably more substantial and poignant than the empty, numerical long-distance blaze of national publicity. He grieved over the coarseness, unkindness, and corruption of our society, and said that "the poet has a peculiar relation to this public. It is unaware of his existence." He said bitterly and light-heartedly that "the gods who had taken away the poet's audience had given him students." Yet he gloried in being a teacher, never apologized for it, and related it to his most serious criticism. Writing of three long poems by Robert Frost, poems too long to include in his essay, he breaks off and says, "I have used rather an odd tone about [these poems] because I feel so much frustration at not being able to quote and go over them, as I so often have done with friends and classes." Few critics could so gracefully descend from the grand manner or be so offhand about their dignity. His essays are never encrusted with the hardness of a professor. They have the raciness and artistic gaiety of his own hypnotic voice.

* * *

Jarrell was the most readable and generous of critics of contemporary poetry. His novel, *Pictures from an Institution*, whatever its fictional oddities, is a unique and serious joke book. How often I've met people who keep it by their beds or somewhere handy, and read random pages aloud to lighten their hearts. His book *A Sad Heart at the Supermarket* had a condescending press. When one listened to these social essays, they were like *dies irae* sermons, strange ones that cauterized the soul, and yet made us weep with laughter. A banal world found them banal. But what Jarrell's inner life really was — all its wonder, variety, and subtlety is best told in his poetry. To the end, he was writing with deepening force, clarity, and frankness. For some twenty-five years he wrote excellent poems.

*   *
    *

It all comes back to me now — the just under thirty years of our friendship, mostly meetings in transit, mostly in Greensboro, North Carolina, the South he loved and stayed with, though no agrarian, but a radical liberal. Poor modern-minded exile from the forests of Grimm, I see him unbearded, slightly South American-looking, then later bearded, with a beard we at first wished to reach out our hands to and pluck off, but which later became him, like Walter Bagehot's, or some Symbolist's in France's *fin de siècle* Third Republic. Then unbearded again. I see the bright, petty, pretty sacred objects he accumulated for his joy and solace: Vermeer's red-hatted girl, the Piero and Donatello reproductions, the photographs of his bruised, merciful heroes: Chekhov, Rilke, Marcel Proust. I see the white sporting Mercedes-Benz, the ever better cut and most deliberately jaunty clothes, the television with its long afternoons of professional football, those matches he thought miraculously more graceful than college football.... Randall had an uncanny clairvoyance for helping friends in subtle precarious moments — almost always as only he could help, with something written: critical sentences in a letter, or an unanticipated published book review. Twice or thrice, I think, he must have thrown me a lifeline. In his own life, he had much public acclaim and more private. The public, at least, fell cruelly short of what he deserved. Now that he is gone, I see clearly that the spark from heaven really struck and irradiated the lines and being of my dear old friend — his noble, difficult, and beautiful soul.

Carl Sandburg
1878–1967

by

WILLIAM SAROYAN

I REMEMBER our first meeting, in San Francisco, at the bookstore owned and operated by Leon Gelber and Theodore Lilienthal, on Sutter Street, in 1937, exactly thirty years ago, when you were fifty-nine, which is my present age, and I was twenty-nine.... It was Leon who told me one summer afternoon when I walked into the store on Sutter Street, "Carl Sandburg's in the back room, do you want to meet him?"

And so we met. I suggested we go to a bar on Turk Street for a drink because John Garfield was going to join me there. With John Garfield was somebody else, also a writer, and quite famous at the time, at least in Hollywood, but for the life of me I can't remember his name.

After two drinks at Joe Bailey's, where I used to play stud, you asked about the Cliff House, so we left the saloon and got into a taxi and drove out Geary to the Cliff House for a couple more drinks, all the while watching the seals on Seal Rock, and the ebb and flow of the ocean around the Rock.

Then, we took a taxi back to town, to Joe Vanessi's on Broadway near Pacific for some good Italian food. You were older than the rest of us, but you did just fine — talking, drinking, eating, and looking exactly the way you do in your photographs, exactly the way a poet ought to look — that is, simultaneously special, different, unique, but at the same time also casual, commonplace, and one of the people. The straw-colored hair of your head always stayed just a little awry, uncombed, apparently ignored.

Around eleven, after the Italian food and wine, we broke up, having all of us had a rather nice time. That is to say, you went home somewhere, to a hotel or to somebody's house where you were staying, and the writer whose name I can't remember said he had a big day tomorrow, and he began to walk home, and Garfield and I went up to Izzy's on Pacific Street.

"Imagine it," Garfield said, "a great man like that, a famous poet, an old guy, loafing around with a couple of kids from the slums, talking with us, drinking with us, eating with us, as if he were a kid from the slums, too. When I get to be his age I only hope I can be that young."

*　　*
　*

Well, John Garfield died at the age of forty or so, at the height of a sensationally successful career as a movie star, and the writer whose name I can't remember, who was also a little under thirty when we all met, has faded away, which is either the same as dying or worse. And a lot of new poets and actors and story-writers have come along and taken their places among their kind, the new poets moving in the direction of Ezra Pound, T. S. Eliot, William Carlos Williams, and Wallace Stevens; the new actors taking their places beside Clark Gable, Humphrey Bogart, James Cagney, Paul Muni, Spencer Tracy, and Cary Grant; and the new story-writers moving in the direction of Ernest Hemingway, Scott Fitzgerald, William Faulkner, Morley Callaghan, and Stephen Vincent Benét.

That *was* America, in short. That was innocent America, or ignorant America, or confused America. And always, no matter how the history of the nation changed, or what happened in Europe and Asia, or who arrived or who departed, there was news in the press about Carl Sandburg, and a photograph, so that I was reminded of our happy hours one summer day and night in San Francisco long ago.

You played the guitar, you sang "The Blue-Tail Fly," you made records, you went to New York, you went to Hollywood, you gave interviews to newspaper and magazine writers, and at the same time you finished the biggest biography of Abraham Lincoln ever written.

*   *
*

You met several Presidents, and you told me that somebody had approached you about accepting the nomination for the office of President — don't pass it along. Well, you certainly knew more about Lincoln than any other potential Presidential candidate. You met Marilyn Monroe and she loved you like a father. You were a consultant during the filming of the life of Jesus.

Yesterday when I read that you had died at your home in Flat Rock, North Carolina, I felt great sorrow even though you had lived almost nine full decades, had had no failure or frustration, had never been accused of treason, never committed to a hospital for the insane, never been hated, despised, held in contempt, abandoned, hounded, misunderstood, misinterpreted, scorned, belittled, dishonored.

I felt sorry because somewhere along the line the easy

careless fall of the hair on your head, in two mops, right and left, had come to mean to the *people*, to use your term, poetry itself, American poetry, so that you yourself and your poetry and your other writing were taken to be great by the people who do not read poetry, prose, or anything else.

You lived and died famous, but actually unrecognized and unknown. The President himself issued a formal tribute to you which was written by somebody who had made a careful study of your verse. It sounded awfully important but didn't mean anything. You were probably a great man of some sort, but *that* couldn't have been the sort. Not that poets die young, although they do, no matter how long they live. They die real, and contrary to the misconception involved, not once, at the end, but many times right up to the end.

Thomas Merton

1915–1968

by

GUY DAVENPORT

THERE WERE RUMORS a few years ago that Father M.
Louis, OCSO, had retreated even further into his religious
life, and that whereas formerly it was difficult to penetrate
the fastness of the Trappist Monastery at Gethsemani
in Kentucky to see him briefly — a hooded and very holy
figure — it was now impossible. This kind of pious awe
amused Tom Merton immensely, and I once had the fun of
listening to this rumor from an academic type who
reported it as something of a literary state secret. The fun
for me came from the fact that I was able to reply that just
the day before Tom Merton had turned up on my porch in
Lexington, looking for all the world like Jean Genet in
denim jacket and jeans. The rumor had for basis the fact
that after 25 years as a monk, Father Louis had decided to
become a hermit. And who, as he said slyly, was to say
whether a desert father didn't come into town occasionally
to catch up on the news and flip through forbidden magazines? *Poetry*, for instance, in which the Abbot had once
found an offending phrase, was denied him. Nor did the
Trappists subscribe to *The New Yorker*; he found its ads to
be a ready index to the world on which he had turned his

back. As a hermit he had an enviable cabin deep in the woods about a quarter mile from Gethsemani. A black snake lived in the outhouse; it seemed perfectly natural that a snake should share his saintly life. Here he watched the procession of the seasons, wrote his poems and his books, and received visitors. Theology and poetry made up the library. Visitors were usually instructed to bring beer; he would produce from various frugal cloths a goat cheese, a loaf, and salted peanuts. And afterwards, from under the bed, he would triumphantly bring out a rather far-gone bottle of bourbon, "to keep the cold out of the bones."

What one could not suspect from Tom Merton's writing was the boyish happiness of the man. He seemed to live in that peace which must come after a final subduing of the selfishness which holds us back from God. He had become a Trappist to be himself, for he knew that the self the world had shaped of him was not true. If religion meant anything, it meant that God demanded all, and it meant that God had a purpose in demanding all. That is perhaps why there was nothing of the religious about him, nothing ritually pious. He was disarmingly a simple man. He was no guru, and fled from visitors who came to Gethsemani expecting to find a saint with sincere eyes and forgiving hands to lay on their guilt. His very laughter — a laughter robust, medieval, and utterly innocent — would have dashed their image of him. His hermitry is perhaps unique in the history of the Church. He interpreted his new isolation as freedom from the discipline of the monastery and planned wonderful picnics and invited friends to them, specifying women and children as an added luxury.

That he died in Bangkok, of all places, will have been a mystery to the world, as the world did not know that he set

out last summer on a pilgrimage to the East. He had studied the religions of the world for years, and he was fasci-
nated by the contemplative religions of India and Japan. He
had looked in on our own Indians on the way, and fellow
monastics from Kentucky to California. One wonders if the
United States, which he had not seen in thirty ears, was not
as strange to him as the Orient. The week before he died he
had been with Dalai Lama, exiled in India, and they liked
each other. It was impossible not to like Tom Merton. His
writings were not quite what the church always wanted,
and he appeared to be a saint most certainly, but not any
kind of saint one has ever heard of. News of his death has
reached me not by television or radio or newspaper; these
media are too slow, too clogged with the chronicling of fri-
volity and blather to know about the death of a saint in
Bangkok. News has come by telephone, relayed friend by
friend around the world.

Philip Rahv

1901–1973

by

MARY McCARTHY

So he's gone that dear phenomenon. If no two people are alike, he was less like anybody else than anybody. A powerful intellect, a massive, over-powering personality and yet shy, curious, susceptible, confiding. All his life he was sternly faithful to Marxism, for him both a tool of analysis and a wondrous cosmogony; but he loved Henry James and every kind of rich, shimmery, soft texture in literature and in the stuff of experience. He was a resolute modernist, which made him in these recent days old-fashioned. It was as though he came into being with the steam engine: for him, literature began with Dostoevsky and stopped with Joyce, Proust, and Eliot; politics began with Marx, Engels, and stopped with Lenin. He was not interested in Shakespeare, the classics, Greek city-states, and he despised most contemporary writing and contemporary political groups, being grumblingly out of sorts with fashion, except where he felt it belonged — on the backs of good-looking women and girls.

This did not overtake him with age or represent a hardening of his mental arteries. He was always that way. It helped him be a Trotskyite (he was a great admirer of

the Old Man, though never an inscribed adherent) when
Stalinism was chic. Whatever was "in" he threw out with
a snort. Late in his life, serendipity introduced him to the
word "swingers," which summed up everything he was
against. With sardonic relish he adopted it as his personal
shorthand. If he came down from Boston to New York and
went to a literary party and you asked him, "Well, how was
it?" he would answer, "Nothing but swingers!" and give his
short soft bark of a laugh.

Yet he had a gift for discovering young writers. I think
of Saul Bellow, Elizabeth Hardwick, Randall Jarrell, John
Berryman, Bernard Malamud. There were many others. He
was quickly aware of Bob Silvers, editor of *The New York
Review of Books*, and became his close friend — counselor,
too, sometimes. To the end of his life, he remained a friend
of young people. It was middle-aged and old swingers he
held in aversion; young ones, on the whole, he didn't mind.

He had a marvelous sensitivity to verbal phrasing and
structure. What art dealers call "quality" in painting he
would recognize instantly in literature, even of a kind that,
in principle, ought to have been foreign to him. I remember
when I first knew him, back in the mid-thirties, at a time
when he was an intransigent (I thought), pontificating
young Marxist, and I read a short review he had done of
Tender Is the Night — the tenderness of the review, despite
its critical stance, startled me. I could not have suspected
in Rahv that power of sympathetic insight into a writer so
glamorized by rich Americans on the Riviera. Fitzgerald,
I must add, was "out" then and not only for the disagree-
able crowd at the *New Masses*.

*　　*

*

The words *radical* and *modern* had a wonderful charm for Philip; when he spoke them, his sometimes grating tone softened, became reverent, loving, as though touching prayer beads. He was also much attached to the word *ideas*. "He has no ideas," he would declare, dismissing some literary claimant; to be void of ideas was for him the worst disaster that could befall an intellectual. He found this deficiency frequent, almost endemic, among us. That may be why he did not wish to assimilate.

I said, just now, that he was unlike anybody, but now I remember that I have seen someone like him — on the screen. Like the younger Rahv anyway: Serge Bondarchuk, the director of *War and Peace*, playing the part of Pierre. An uncanny resemblance in every sense and unsettling to preconceived notions. I had always pictured Pierre as blond, pink, tall, and fat; nor could I picture Philip as harboring Pierre's ingenuous, embarrassed, puzzled, placid soul — they were almost opposites, I should have thought. And yet that swarthy Russian actor was showing us a different interior Philip and a different exterior Pierre. Saying goodbye to my old friend, I am moved by that and remember his tenderness for Tolstoy (see the very Rahvian and beautiful essay "The Green Twig and the Black Trunk") and Tolstoy's sense of Pierre as the onlooker, the eternal civilian, as out of place at the battle of Borodino in his white hat and green swallowtail coat as the dark little man in his long, dark European clothes eyeing the teacher from behind his grammar school desk in Providence.

Edward Dahlberg
1900–1977

by

WILLIAM O'ROURKE

T HE LAST TIME I spoke with Edward Dahlberg the circumstances were these: I had been living an economically
immature existence, the most lucrative part of which saw
me toiling as a laborer in the South Bronx. You learn only
so much from poverty; it quickly becomes a redundant lesson. I was offered a university position and — always willing to have a new experience — I accepted and thereby
turned into the kind of writer I (and Dahlberg) distrusted:
an author of two books who had a full-time teaching position. My estimation of such an individual had been that he
couldn't possibly be any good. Dahlberg asked me what my
salary was, and I told him. He shouted into the phone: "No
university has ever paid me $12,000!" And he slammed the
receiver down. I hadn't expected those to be my private
version of his last words, but they were. So now in my own
personal ossuary, Dahlberg's stone is etched:

EDWARD DAHLBERG
AMERICAN AUTHOR 1900–1977
"No university has ever
paid me $12,000!"

In the summer of 1978, Crowell brought out his last novel, *The Olive of Minerva or The Comedy of a Cuckold*, and an omnibus volume of his thirties "Proletarian" novels: *Bottom Dogs, From Flushing to Cavalry, Those Who Perish. The Olive of Minerva* was scored in *The New York Times Book Review* by some drone of the academy suffering from terminal snit. He quite fraudulently failed to mention (as did the obituary in the *Times* on February 28, 1977) Dahlberg's masterpiece, the novel-autobiography *Because I Was Flesh.*

I wrote a review of the new book that summer that I now see contained more eulogy than I intended; because I loved the man, it was a difficult task — not, certainly, because there wasn't a good deal to laud.

A good many people had been waiting for him to die. A small cottage industry has developed in the literary world of telling outrageous Dahlberg tales of offense taken and given, of majestic rudeness and sidereal insult. They are of the variety that grows livelier from beyond the grave. The good stories, alas, are often not interred with the bones. So, paraphrasing one of our contemporary heroes of the Reprint Pantheon, What can you say about a seventy-seven-year-old author who has died?

Well, you can say that Edward Dahlberg was a Man of Letters, not of the World. That he was party to no institution that wields power. That he was quite crazy at times, from a combination of drugs and bodily ills. And, that he was always kind to me, even kind enough to suggest that I had plagiarized *Because I Was Flesh.*

In the final five years he began to mimic Lear wild on the heath. The last night, he was up at three in the morning singing television jingles. He found a way of dying quite unlike his life: quietly, in his sleep. Pulmonary congestion.

It would be a sour irony for him if he knew he died in such a Prufrockian manner: "Till human voices wake us, and we drown."

His wife, Julia Lawlor, awoke and discovered him extraordinarily still; she felt his hands and they were cold, and then she felt his feet and they were warm. She did not know if he was dead or in a coma. An electric blanket had kept his feet warm.

The last time I had visited him on East Ninety-first Street we ate Merit Farm chicken, drank beer, and he would alternately rage at me and laugh with me. He had begun to have fierce precariousness of the old that leaves the will and spirit strong, but the body weak. Rage becomes more terrifying because it is apparent that the flesh can no longer endure it.

He fled the city for Ireland and I packed for him his two thousand pounds of books, which was the stone he rolled before him on his travels up and down mountains. I had always wanted a picture of us together, so I borrowed a cheap camera from a friend, and Julia took one of us together dockside. I have the picture; it is two black shapes, one higher than the other. You cannot see his arm around my shoulder.

Quitting Ireland he returned to New York, stayed in the Chelsea, then rented an apartment, much to the distress of a representative of the hotel who wanted him to remain there (hoping, doubtless, for another American author to die under its roof). He abandoned the new place a week later, returned to Ireland, fled back again to the States, and then settled in Santa Barbara, California, where he died. I last saw him amidst the not-yet fading baronic splendor of the Yale Club, where a patron had provided him with quarters. There we shared more laughter and rage. Dahlberg enjoying himself more than he would admit ensconced in the Yale Club's version of WASP heaven. Then came the phone call and the testy ending; Dahlberg did not like simple goodbyes, which is why I'm still shocked that he died in his sleep.

In the preface to the omnibus volume of novels that appeared in 1976, he wrote:

I have commited sundry moldy solecisms; yet I was not born to desecrate literature. Wood that has aged for a thousand years or more becomes charcoal; I have grown old as a result of centuries of sorrows and am just a writer. In a pragmatical era of the polypus that solely reflects its surroundings, I wonder which is more useful nowadays, coal or a good boke.

This is bitter business; and I am angry that a friend has to sing his praises, because it catches in my throat — for any author deserves to have strangers hail him. For whatever Dear Readers there are now, or are to come, Edward Dahlberg wrote eighteen books and one masterpiece that will endure; at the end of his long life he had fewer than six people he would have called "friend."

Muriel Rukeyser
1913–1980

by

DENISE LEVERTOV

MURIEL RUKEYSER, more any other poet I know of (including Pablo Neruda), consistently fused lyricism and overt social and political concern. Her *Collected Poems*, which came out just over a year before her death, clearly reveals this seamlessness, this wholeness: virtually every page contains questions or affirmations relating to her sense of the humane creature as a social species with the responsibilities, culpabilities, and possibilities attendant upon that condition. And virtually every page is infused with the sonic and figurative qualities of lyric poetry.

Her life presented a parallel fusion. From her presence as a protester at the Scottsboro trial in 1931, when she was eighteen, to the lone journey to Seoul which she undertook in 1975 in the (alas, unsuccessful) attempt — using her prestige as president of P E N — to obtain the release from jail of Kim Chi Ha, the Korean poet and activist, Muriel *acted* on her beliefs, rather than assuming that the ability to verbalize them somehow exempted her from further responsibility. The range of her concern expressed the fact that she went beyond humanitarian sympathy to a recognition of interconnections and parallels: she had a strong, independent personal grasp of politics, and just as she blended the engaged and the lyrical, the life of writing and the life of action, so too did she blend her warm compassion and her extraordinary intelligence. To list some of the subjects of her poems is also to allude to events of her biography, and vice versa: Spain during the civil war; the working conditions of West Virginia miners in the 1930s; the unhating, profoundly civilized spirit of Hanoi, 1972; war-resistance and jail in D. C. — these are a few instances that come to mind. Whether working with schoolchildren in Harlem or learning to fly a plane, whether experiencing single-parenthood or researching the life of the sixteenth–seventeenth-century mathematician Thomas Harriot, Muriel never placed the objects of her attention in the sealed compartments of sterile expertise, but informed all that she touched with that unifying imagination that made her truly great.

Something that especially moves me about Muriel Ruskeyser is the way in which her work moved towards greater economy and clarity in her later books. There are marvelous early poems, but sometimes her very generosity of spirit seemed to bring about a rush of words that had not the condensed power she eventually attained. Clarity of communication was not easy for her because her mind was so complex, causing her conversation often to be hard to follow as she leapt across gulfs most of us had to trudge down into and up the other side; but she did attain it — a luminous precison — time after time.

I had known Muriel for many years before she and I and Jane Hart went to Vietnam together in the fall of 1972. That journey bound us in a deeper friendship.

Among my recollections are two small incidents from

that trip that seem expressive: one is her painful embarrassment at having to receive medical attention in a Hanoi
hospital — she felt that among so many war-injured Vietnamese civilians, an American with an injured toe was
grossly out of place. (In fact, the matter was serious because
of her diabetes.) The other is the look of distress I suddenly
noticed on her face when I, in answer to a question from
one of the Vietnamese writers we met, described New York
City in extremely negative terms. She was a New Yorker
born and bred and though she knew all about its terrors
and tragedies, she loved the city and saw its possibilities,
looking upon it with passionate hope, as upon a troubled
but beloved person.

It would be inappropriate to memorialize her, however
briefly, without mentioning her humor. (She included in
her last book the two-line squib,

> *I'd rather be Muriel*
> *than be dead and be Ariel,*

under the title *Not to be Printed, Not to be Said, Not to be
Thought.*) Equally inappropriate would be omission of a
reference to her lifelong interest in science and to the fact
that she wrote not only poetry (including translations) but
notable biographies, children's books, and two other uncat-
egorizable prose works. *The Life of Poetry* and *The Orgy.*
Then, too, there was her life as a teacher, for many years,
at Sarah Lawrence, where the tutorial system demands of
faculty an unusual degree of dedication.

The loss of this person, this poet, and for some of us
this wonderful friend, is a great one. Her work and her
example remain to sustain us — an ongoing source of life-

affirmative energy. In the preface to her *Collected Poems* she wrote of "the parts of life in which we dive deep and sometimes — with strength of expression and skill and luck — reach that place where things are shared, and we all recognize the secrets." Muriel Rukeyser had that strength, that skill, that luck — and she did reach that place.

Katherine Anne Porter

1890–1980

by

ROBERT PENN WARREN

AFTER A LONG and painful sequel to a stroke, with increasing impairment of faculties, but with occasional flashes of old charm and wit, Katherine Anne Porter's prayer for death is answered. A famous, though far from massive, body of published work is her most obvious legacy. But there is also an enormous body of correspondence (she was a compulsive writer of letters to all sorts of people, in a style headlong, witty, shrewd, or eloquent) and a number of private journals that await editing and publication. It would, in fact, seem that experience could scarcely exist for her until it had found its "word."

Pondering this extraordinary accumulation of spontaneous and unpublished material, one is tempted to suggest that for Katherine Anne Porter the distinction between art and life was never arbitrarily drawn: Life found its fulfillment in the thrust toward art, and art sprang from life as realized in meditation. In an interview with Hank Lopez, she once said: "Everything I ever wrote in the way of fiction is based very securely on something in real life." Eudora Welty sensed this about her friend when she wrote, "What we are responding to in Katherine Anne Porter's work is the intensity of its life."

This insistence on "life" by both the author and her critics seems to be an invitation to the study of the "life" as available in correspondences, journals, and other more random sources. But here, a caveat. The life of a dedicated writer who happens to be a charming, beautiful, tough-minded, and witty woman, a brilliant conversationalist, a convincing judge of character, a friend of the great and the obscure, a wanderer in many countries and many sections of this country, would seem to be a natural prey for the popular biographer who aims for a quick kill and a brief glory near the top of the best-sellers. It is conceivable that Katherine Anne Porter might even risk the fate that, in reference to Katherine Mansfield, she has called the worst "that an artist can suffer — to be overwhelmed by her own legend, to have her work neglected for an interest in her 'personality.'"

No exploration of Katherine Anne Porter's "personality," however, can explain the success of her art: the scrupulous and expressive intricacy of structure, the combination of a precision of language, the revealing shock of precise observation and organic metaphor, a vital rhythmic felicity of style, and a significant penetration of a governing idea into the remotest details of a work. If, as V. S. Pritchett has put it, the writer of short stories is concerned with "one thing that implies many" — or much — then we have here a most impressive artist.

How did Katherine Anne Porter transmute life finally into art? In her journal of 1936, she herself provided a most succinct, simple, and precise answer to my question. All her experience, she writes, seems to be simply in memory, with continuity, marginal notes, constant revision and comparison of one thing with another. But now comes the last phase, that of ultimate transmutation: "Now and again, thousands of memories converge, harmonize, arrange themselves around a central idea in a coherent form, and I write a story."

The author here speaks as though each story were an isolated creation, called into being by the initial intuition of a theme. That, indeed, may have been her immediate perception of the process of composition. The work of any serious writer, however, is not a grab bag, but a struggle, conscious or unconscious, for a meaningful unity, a unity that can be recorded in terms of temperament or theme. In my view, the final importance of Katherine Anne Porter is not merely that she has written a number of fictions remarkable for both grace and strength, a number of fictions which have enlarged and deepened the nature of the story, both short and long, in our time, but that she has created an *œuvre* — a body of work including fiction, essays, letters, and journals — that bears the stamp of a personality distinctive, delicately perceptive, keenly aware of the depth and darkness of human experience, delighted by the beauty of the world and the triumphs of human kindness and warmth, and thoroughly committed to a quest for meaning in the midst of the ironic complexities of man's lot.

John Cheever

1912–1982

by

SAUL BELLOW

Jᴏʜɴ ᴀɴᴅ I met at irregular intervals all over the U.S. I
gave him lunch in Cambridge, he bought me a drink in
Palo Alto, he came to Chicago, I went to New York. Our
friendship, a sort of hydroponic plant, flourished in the air.
It was, however, healthy, fed by good elements, and it was
a true friendship. Because we met in transit, as it were, we
lost no time in getting down to basics. On both sides there
was instant candor. The speed at which necessary information was exchanged was wonderfully amusing. Each of
us knew what the other was up to. We worked at the same
trade, which, in America, is a singularly odd and difficult
one, practiced by difficult people who are not always
pleased by the talents of their contemporaries (Think of
that wicked wizard the late Nabokov, who coined terms like
"ethnopsychic novelists," dismissing us by the platoon.)
John was not in the least grudging or rivalrous. Like John
Berryman, he was fabulously generous with other writers.
Yes, an odd lot, poets and writers of fiction. And to those
who write novels about it, the country, too, is singularly
paradoxical, very different from the "normal" America that

businessmen, politicians, journalists, trade unionists, advertising men and scientists, engineers and farmers, live in.

I think that the differences between John and me endeared us to each other more than the affinities. He was a Yankee; I, from Chicago, was the son of Jewish immigrants. His voice, his style, his humor, were different from mine. His manner was reticent, mine was ... something else. It fell to John to resolve these differences. He did this without the slightest difficulty, simply by putting human essences in first place: first the persons — himself, myself — and after that the other stuff — class origins, social history. A fairly experienced observer, I have never seen the thing done as he did it — done, I mean, as if it were not done at all. It flowed directly from his nature. And although his manner was reticent, there was nothing that John would not say about himself. When he seemed to hesitate he was actually condensing his judgments, his opinions, his estimates of his own accomplishments, in order to give them greater force. He spoke of himself as he would speak of anybody else, disinterestedly and concisely. He preferred short views and practiced the same economy in speech as in writing. He might have said, as Pushkin, did, "I live as I write; I write as I live."

Miss Kakutani of the *New York Times* used excellent judgment in choosing the quotation with which she began John's obituary: "The constants that I look for," he once wrote, "are a love of light and a determination to trace some moral chain of being." I'm sure that John didn't relish making statements about morals and being; that wasn't his style. I see it as a reluctant assertion, something he had at last to say to correct distortion by careless readers, book reviewers, and academic category makers. I suppose that he felt it necessary at last to try to say what he had been doing with himself for some fifty years.

There are writers whose last novels are very like the first. Having learned their trade, mastered it once and for all, they practice it with little variation to the very end. They can be very good novelists. Think of Somerset Maugham or Arnold Bennett (you can supply American names of your own), exceedingly proficient and dependable servants of the reading public. What they lack is the impulse to expand. They do not develop; they seldom surprise. John Cheever was a writer of another sort altogether. He was one of the self-transformers. The reader of his collected stories witnesses a dramatic metamorphosis. The second half of the collection is quite different from the first. Rereading him, as I have recently done, it became apparent to me, and will certainly be evident to anyone who reads him attentively, how much of his energy went into self-enlargement and transformation and how passionate the investment was. It is extraordinarily moving to find the inmost track of a man's life and to decipher the signs he has left us. Although the subjects and themes of his stories did not change much, he wrote with deepening power and feeling.

With characteristic brevity and diffidence, he only tells us, toward the end, that he loved the light and that he was determined to trace some moral chain of being — no simple matter in a world that, in his own words, lies "spread out around us like a bewildered and stupendous dream." His intention was, however, not only to find evidence of a moral life in a disorderly society but also to give us the poetry of the bewildering and stupendously dreamlike world in which we find ourselves. There are few people around who set themselves such a task, who put their souls to work in such a way. "Normal America" might ask, if it were inclined to formulate such a question, "What sense does *that* actually make?" Perhaps not much, as "sense" is commonly defined. But there are other definitions. For me no one makes more sense, no one is so interesting, as a man who engages his soul in an enterprise of this kind. I find myself, as I grow older, increasingly drawn to those who live as John did. Those who choose such an enterprise, who engage in such a struggle, make all the interest of life for us. The life John led leaves us in his debt. We are his debtors, and we are indebted to him even for the quality of the pain we feel at his death.

by

ROBERT CREELEY

T ED BERRIGAN'S DEATH leaves a hole of adamant loss.
There won't be another like him, ever, and what's left as
always to do is to remember that, and what his writing was
all about, and how, with such disarming simpleness, it could
hold the largest imagination of human relationships and
the world in which they are given to be.

Robert Duncan spoke of him as a genius of *pathos,* a
power that could move the heart so commonly, simply, as in
one of his great poems, "Things to Do in Providence." His
insistent ritualizing of his friends' names, his lovely re-
hearsal of them, often as a poem would begin, to make the
company of his life become the place where all authority of
speech might then occur — what a generous *and* American
act! I recall a British friend's irritation on hearing him do
this, at a reading he gave with Jim Dine in London years ago
("Ted/is ready./The bell/rings. . ."). And saying something
like, "I don't know those people. . . ." She missed the point
altogether because Ted would dearly have liked her to know
them — they were the greatest friends in the world.

He *was* an Irishman from Providence, which always
moved me. Together with Charles Olson and John Wieners,

he was my particular New England — certainly all I ever knew or believed in. I loved the way he took on New York and not only made it but so permeated its New York style, like they say, that I do think he's finally as evident in that manner of poetry as is Frank O'Hara, whose work he so loved. But the pace and rhythm of his poems, the seemingly open way of the words, the commonness of them, the literal action of what happens, the content at once so obvious and so resonant, all that is inimitable, however large the appetite now to possess it.

Then, as with Mr. Wieners, he remains forever in mind as a great gentleman, an exceptional one. He taught manners and common caring, by his own example. Despite he was a hard man to interrupt(!), he certainly heard you. I remember my own applications to his attention got always a courteous reception and response. He had great honor — put most simply as he did, "Give it your best shot..." "I'd like to take the whole trip..." He made an extensive, particular, possible world of his life and lived there difficulty sans complaint.

The raw shock of his death, no matter he or anyone else expected it, makes no room now for spelling it out further. You will hear his wild tremulous wistful reflective engaging way of saying it in any work of his that you read or hear him reading. Thankfully there is the substantial collection of his poems, *So Going Around Cities*, and the reissued *Sonnets*, and much else. It won't bring him back but it's what he left, solid as a rock.

James Baldwin
1924–1987

by

TONI MORRISON

Jᴏᴍᴍʏ. There is too much to think about you, and too much to feel. The difficulty is your life refuses summation — it always did — and invites contemplation instead. Like many of us left here I thought I knew you. Now I discover that in your company it is myself I know. That is the astonishing gift of your art and your friendship. You gave us ourselves to think about, to cherish. We are like Hall Montana watching "with new wonder" his brother saints, knowing the song he sang is us. "He is us."

I never heard a single command from you, yet the demands you made on me, the challenges you issued to me, were nevertheless unmistakable, even if unenforced: that I work and think at the top of my form, that I stand on moral ground but know that ground must be shored up by mercy, that "the world is before [me] and [I] need not take it or leave it as it was when [I] came in."

Well, the season was always Christmas with you there and, like one aspect of that scenario, you did not neglect to bring at least three gifts. You gave me a language to dwell in, a gift so perfect it seems my own invention. I have been thinking your spoken and written thoughts for so long I believed they were mine. I have been seeing the world through your eyes for so long, I believed that clear, clear view was my own. Even now, even here, I need you to tell me what I am feeling and how to articulate it. So I have pored again through the 6,895 pages of your published work to acknowledge the debt and thank you for the credit. No one possessed or inhabited language for me the way you did. You made American English honest — genuinely international. You exposed its secrets and reshaped it until it was truly modern, dialogic, representative, humane. You stripped it of ease and false comfort and fake innocence and evasion and hypocrisy. And in place of deviousness was clarity. In place of soft, plump lies was lean, targeted power. In place of intellectual disingenuousness and what you called "exasperating egocentricity," you gave us undecorated truth. You replaced lumbering platitudes with an upright elegance. You went into that forbidden territory and decolonized it, "robbed it of the jewel of its naïveté," and un-gated it for black people so that in your wake we could enter it, occupy it, restructure it in order to accommodate our complicated passion — not our vanities but our intricate, difficult, demanding beauty, our tragic, insistent knowledge, our lived reality, our sleek classical imagination — all the while refusing "to be defined by a language that has never been able to recognize [us]." In your hands language was handsome again. In your hands we saw how it was meant to be: neither bloodless nor bloody, and yet alive.

It infuriated some people. Those who saw the paucity of their own imagination in the two-way mirror you held up to them attacked the mirror, tried to reduce it to fragments which they could then rank and grade, tried to dismiss the shards where your image and theirs remained — locked but ready to soar. You are an artist after all and an artist is forbidden a career in this place; an artist is permitted only a commercial hit. But for thousands and thousands of those who embraced your text and who gave themselves permission to hear your language, by that very gesture they ennobled themselves, became unshrouded, civilized.

The second gift was your courage, which you let us share: the courage of one who could go as a stranger in the village and transform the distances between people into intimacy with the whole world; courage to understand that experience in ways that made it a personal revelation for each of us. It was you who gave us the courage to appropriate an alien, hostile, all-white geography because you had discovered that "this world (meaning history) is white no longer and it will never be white again." Yours was the courage to live life in and from its belly as well as beyond its edges, to see and say what it was, to recognize and identify evil but never tear or stand in awe of it. It is a courage that came from a ruthless intelligence married to a pity so profound it could convince anyone who cared to know that those who despised us "need the moral authority of their former slaves, who are the only people in the world who know anything about them and who may be, indeed, the only people in the world who really care anything about them." When that unassailable combination of mind and heart, of intellect and passion was on display it guided us through treacherous landscape as it did when you wrote these words every rebel, every dissident, revolutionary, every practicing artist from Capetown to Poland from Waycross to Dublin memorized: "A person does not lightly elect to oppose his society. One would much rather be at home among one's compatriots than be mocked and detested by them. And there is a level on which the mockery of the people, even their hatred, is moving, because it is so blind: it is terrible to watch people cling to their captivity and insist on their own destruction."

The third gift was hard to fathom and even harder to accept. It was your tenderness — a tenderness so delicate I thought it could not last, but last it did and envelop me it did. In the midst of anger it tapped me lightly like the child in Tish's womb: "Something almost as hard to catch as a whisper in a crowded place, as light and as definite as a spider's web, strikes below my ribs, stunning and astonishing my heart . . . the baby, turning for the first time in its incredible veil of water, announces its presence and claims me; tells me, in that instant, that what can get worse can get better . . . in the meantime — forever — it is entirely up to me." Yours was a tenderness, a vulnerability, that asked everything, expected everything and, like the world's own Merlin, provided us with the ways and means to deliver. I suppose that is why I was always a bit better behaved around you, smarter, more capable, wanting to be worth the love you lavished, and wanting to be steady enough to witness the pain you had witnessed and were tough enough to bear while it broke your heart, wanting to be generous enough to join your smile with one of my own, and reckless enough to jump on in that laugh you laughed. Because our joy and our laughter were not only all right, they were necessary.

You knew, didn't you, how I needed your language and the mind that formed it? How I relied on your fierce courage to tame wildernesses for me? How strengthened I was by the certainty that came from knowing you would never hurt me? You knew, didn't you, how I loved your love? You knew. This then is no calamity. No. This is jubilee. "Our crown," you said, "has already been bought and paid for. All we have to do," you said, "is wear it."

And we do, Jimmy. You crowned us.

by

EDWARD HOAGLAND

EDWARD ABBEY, who died in March at the age of 62, seemed, at his best, the nonpareil "nature writer" of recent decades. It was a term he came to detest, a term used to pigeonhole and marginalize some of the most intriguing American writers who are dealing with matters central to us — yet it can be a ticket to oblivion in the bookstores. Joyce Carol Oates, for instance, in a slapdash though interesting essay called "Against Nature," speaks of nature writers' "painfully limited set of responses ... REVERENCE, AWE, PIETY, MYSTICAL ONENESS." She must never have read Edward Abbey; yet it was characteristic of him that for an hour of two, he might have agreed.

He wrote with exceptional exactitude and an unusually honest and logical understanding of causes and consequences, but he also loved argument, churlishness and exaggeration. Personally, he was a labyrinth of anger and generosity, shy but arresting because of his mixture of hillbilly and cowboy qualities, and even when silent he appeared bigger than life. He had hitchhiked from Appalachia for the first time at age 17 to what became an immediate love match with the West, and, I'm sure, slept out more nights under the stars than all of his current competitors combined. He was uneven and self-indulgent as a writer and often scanted his talent by working too fast, but he had about him an authenticity that springs from the page and is beloved by a rising generation of readers, who have enabled his early collection of rambles, *Desert Solitaire* (1968), to run through 18 printings in mass-market paperback. His fine comic novel, *The Monkey Wrench Gang* (1975), has sold half a million copies. Both books, indeed, have inspired a new eco-guerilla environmental organization called Earth First!, whose other patron saint is Ned Ludd (from whom the Luddites took their name), though it's perhaps no more radical than John Muir's Sierra Club appeared to be when that organization was formed in 1892.

Like many good writers, Abbey dreamed of producing "the fat masterpiece," as he called the "nubble" that he had worked on for the past dozen years and that was supposed to boil everything down to a thousand pages or so. When edited in half, it came out last fall as *The Fool's Progress*, an autobiographical yarn that lunges cross-country several times, full of apt descriptions and antic fun — *Ginger Man* stuff — though not with the coherence or poignance he had hoped for. A couple of his other novels hold up fairly well, too: *Black Sun* and *The Brave Cowboy*, which came out in movie form starring Kirk Douglas and Walter Matthau in 1962 (*Lonely Are the Brave*) and brought Abbey a munificent $7,500.

*   *
*

Abbey was a writer who liked to play poker with cowboys, while continuing to ridicule the ranch owners who overgraze the West's ravaged grasslands. The memorial picnic for him in Saguaro National Monument outside Tucson, Ariz., went on for 12 hours, and besides the readings performed with rock-bottom affection there was beer-drinking, love-making, gunfire and music, much as he had hoped. The potluck stew was from two "slow elk" as he liked to call beef cattle poached from particularly greedy entrepreneurs on the public's wildlands. He was an egalitarian, he said — by which he meant that he believed all wildlife and the full panoply of natural vegetation have a right to live equal to man's — and these beeves had belonged to a cowman who specialized in hounding Arizona's scarce mountain lions.

Abbey died of internal bleeding from a circulatory disorder, with a few weeks' notice of how sick he was. Two days before the event he decided to leave the hospital, wishing to die in the desert; at sunup he had himself disconnected from the tubes and machinery. His wife Clarke and three friends drove him as far out of town as his condition allowed. They built a campfire for him to look at, until, feeling death at hand, he crawled into his sleeping bag with Clarke. But by noon, finding he was still alive and possibly better, he asked to be taken home and placed on a mattress on the floor of his writing cabin. There he said his gentle goodbyes.

His written instructions were that he should be "transported in the bed of a pickup truck" deep into the desert and buried anonymously, wrapped in his sleeping bag, in the beautiful spot where his grave would never be found, with "lots of rocks" piled on top to keep the coyotes off. Abbey of course loved coyotes (and, for that matter, buzzards) and had played his flute to answer their howls during the many years he had earned his living watching for fires from Government towers on the Grand Canyon's North Rim, on Aztec Peak in Tonto National Forest and in Glacier National Park before he finally won tenure as a "fool professor" at the University of Arizona. His friend who was the model for G. W. Hayduke in *The Monkey Wrench Gang* was squatting beside him on the floor as his life ebbed away. "Hayduke" is actually a legend in his own right in parts of the West, a sort or contemporary mountain man who returned to town as to a calving ground several years ago when he wanted to have and raise children. The last smile that crossed Abbey's face was when "Hayduke" told him were he would be put.

The place is, inevitably, a location where mountain lions, antelope, big-horn sheep, deer and javelinas leave tracks, where owls, poor-wills and coyotes hoot and cacomistles scratch, with a range of stiff terrain overhead and grease-wood, rabbitbrush, ocotillo and noble old cactuses about. First seven, then ten buzzards gathered while the grave was being dug; as he had wished, it was a rocky spot. One man jumped into the hole to be sure it felt O. K. before laying Abbey in, and afterward in a kind of reprise of the antic spirit that animates *The Monkey Wrench Gang*, and that should make anybody but a developer laugh out loud, went around heaping up false rockpiles at ideal gravesites throughout the Southwest, because this last peaceful act of outlawry of Abbey's was the gesture of legend and there will be seekers for years to come.

*   *
*

Last year a paean to Abbey's work in *National Review* finished with a quote from a passage in Faulkner: "Oleh, Chief. Grandfather." To which we can add Amen. But instead

let's close with a bit of Ed Abbey, from a minor book called
Appalachian Wilderness (1970), which foretold why he
chose that lost grave where he lies:

*How strange and wonderful is our home, our earth, with its
swirling vaporous atmosphere, its flowing and frozen climbing
creatures, the croaking things with wings that hang on rocks and
soar through fog, the furry grass, the scaly seas . . . how utterly
rich and wild. . . . Yet some among us have the nerve, the inso-
lence, the brass, the gall to whine about the limitations of our
earthbound fate and yearn for some more perfect world beyond
the sky. We are none of us good enough for the world we have.*

Mary McCarthy
1912–1989

by

JOHN LEONARD

I AM ... IN MOURNING for Mary McCarthy.... *Time* magazine once called her "quite possibly the cleverest woman America has ever produced." It isn't clear whether *Time* means this as an insult. To call a person clever implies a "merely"; she might have been something grander; she isn't entirely serious. On the other hand, clever is what *Time* magazine has always wanted most in the world to be, so maybe they thought they were being nice.

She was clever, ferociously so. And wicked, too. This country loves a Bad Girl, at least one at a time, like Cher. When McCarthy came out of the American West, after a wretched Dickensian childhood, to Vassar and then to New York in the '30s, she must have seemed to the West Side intellectuals, worrying their Marx and Freud, a kind of '20s throwback, a flapper with brains. "A princess among trolls." The reviews she wrote for *The Nation* and *The New Republic* were a kind of SOS magic scouring pad on the brainpan of the culture; we saw the reflection of her grin.

When she moved in with Philip Rahv, he put her to work for *Partisan Review*, reviewing plays. Poor Clifford Odets! When she left Philip Rahv, it was to move in with Edmund

Wilson, who encouraged her to write fiction. I doubt he expected himself to turn up in this fiction. Nor could Rahv, Dwight Macdonald, Harold Taylor, etc., have been pleased when they, too, turned up, the living dead. About her novels she once explained, "What I do is take real plums and put them in an imaginary cake."

You must understand that I grew up reading *The Nation*, *The New Republic* and, especially, *Partisan Review*. (In this southern California boyhood, I also subscribed to the *Congressional Record* so I'd have someone to talk to each afternoon when I came home from school.) The intellectuals of the anti-Stalinist Left, the heavyweights of psychoanalysis and modernist literature, were my heroes. In those days, there was a coherent literary culture, and its avatars actually talked to one another. Until I read the satiric novels of Mary McCarthy — swam in the ice blue water of her disdain — it hadn't occurred to me that they also went to bed with one another, just like Gore Vidal and Jack Kerouac . . . and embarrassed themselves.

That some of them had gone to bed with McCarthy was delicious but also frightening. She would know more than they did, like Doris Lessing and Simone de Beauvoir. She was my first crush. Years later, when I did meet her at various Manhattan jolly-ups, she was, of course, kind but firm. Like Lionel Trilling and Hannah Arendt, she took it upon herself to instruct me in my duty, but made it clear there wasn't enough time to learn even half of what she'd already forgotten. It is bitter now to contemplate the handful of letters I have from her. Each blue aerogram from Paris reproves me for some critical or ideological delinquency.

If her novels lack the generosity of great literature, they are full of everything else that counts, like people, places,

plots and ideas; money, honor, betrayal and sex; a wonderful nineteenth-century energetic curiosity. *Memories of a
Catholic Girlhood* is as good as memoirs get. *Venice
Observed* and *The Stones of Florence* are travel-writing mas-
terpieces. Her essay on Nabokov's *Pale Fire* is a classic, and
her defense of Arendt against the critics of *Eichmann in
Jerusalem* was brave and brilliant. In her books on Vietnam,
on Watergate and on terrorism, she followed a blood red
moral thread through the labyrinth 'of a totalitarian century. She read everything, and was indignant about everything, and, yes, clever about everything.

What I'll miss most is her faith that we can know the
world, and choose what we make of ourselves in that world,
and maybe even save it. Literature is publicity now, and
politics are public relations. I'd love to have been in New
York back then, when she first arrived from the West, from
the Moon, this Diana, this huntress. But I was born too
late. Damn.

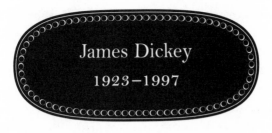

James Dickey

1923–1997

by

REYNOLDS PRICE

JAMES DICKEY was a member of that puzzling and self-punishing tribe of American writers — a tribe that included Hemingway, Faulkner, and Robert Frost — who wanted the public to think they were anything but artists. As Hemingway was the big-game hunter, Faulkner the gentleman farmer and rider to hounds, and Frost the cracker-barrel codger, so Jim Dickey worked hard to be taken for an archer, a country guitarist, a lady-killer, or a Viking berserker stoked with mead. Anyone who spent more than two consecutive days in the Dickey presence, however, knew that — at least as much as Hemingway, whose sensibility was as delicate as eggshell — Dickey was an artist, a poet to the utter bone.

He never forgot that he and I first met on the day of Evelyn Waugh's death — April 10, 1966. No matter how often we encountered each other in the three ensuing decades, even in chance airport passings, Jim would generally get around to asking me if I remembered the day we met. And even when I'd say yes, he'd always tell me again: "You walked in that door, black-haired as a crow, held out your hand to me and said, 'Evelyn Waugh just died.' I knew right then I was going to like you."

In 1966 Jim and I were both young and in good health. I was 33 and had just published my second novel, *A Generous Man*. Jim was a decade older and on the verge of receiving the National Book Award for his splendid volume of poems *Buckdancer's Choice*. He'd come to read at Duke University, where I still teach; and that reading was my first exposure to a riveting power I'd never seen or heard previously from a poet, though I'd heard some great ones — Frost and Auden, for instance, several times each.

Some of Jim's power was that of a practiced snake-oil salesman — his dancer's command of an immense head and body, his shamelessly explicit delight in the brilliance of his own poetry and his baritone mastery of its delivery, the intensity of his gaze, which sooner or later seemed to lock on to every face in the audience and speak to that face alone. Back home, though, you could take down his books, read the poems to yourself in silence, and find them as deeply resonant and sturdily built as he'd claimed them to be. (Occasionally, when he read a lesser poem, his vivid prefatory anecdote about its occasion would prove more memorable than the poem.) You could hear, beneath Jim's lines, both the startling freshness with which his own past was metamorphosed into live verse and the echoes from his endless reading in older European and American poets. You could see the originality with which those lessons were deployed, and the honor that was done those masters in the grateful transaction. You could read Jim's baldly candid essays about other poets and witness again that same genuine reverence for the power of preternatural human attentiveness and the language it makes from its watching.

Those three decades ago, Jim was still a Gypsy poet. He'd yet to settle into his final secure position at the University of South Carolina. He taught his last class there, with portable oxygen, only a few days before his death in January. Meanwhile he'd taught well and hard at various smaller institutions across the country; he toured ceaselessly to collect the tiny sums on which even the best poets then supported themselves. (In the late 1950's Auden said to me, "I never open my mouth for less than $300.") And as Jim and I met often through the remainder of the '60s and thereafter, I was soon wondering — as I've done with more than a few of my other poet friends — if those itinerant begging years of Jim's hadn't jarred some fragile internal gyrostabilizer that would never again quite steady itself.

Endless nights in the saloons of chain motels after your 500th punch-and-cookies English department reception are not the nursery of serious poetic brooding and radiant deliveries. I'd heard Dylan Thomas read at Duke in my own undergraduate years, six months before his sudden death at 39; and early in our acquaintance Jim Dickey was giving me and many of his other admiring friends cause to wonder if he would make it out of his 40s. But however loaded, elated, or exhausted, Jim through our 30 years of friendship continued unfailingly to meet me with a detailed, alert kindness and the plainly informed encouragement that a younger writer so often fails to get from an elder.

Given his looming size, Dickey's kindness could have its strikingly original moments. I recall an otherwise decorous party at Peter Taylor's at which Jim — having given a lengthy and almost alarmingly accurate imitation of Marlon Brando — then proceeded for no apparent reason to

lift me suddenly off the floor (I weighed 175 pounds),
carry me nimbly across the room, deposit me in an arm-
chair and say, "I've never done so but if I were ever to sleep
with a man, I'd want it to be either you or Ned Rorem." Or
there was the evening backstage at the Library of Congress, as Jim was about to introduce a reading by me and
John Cheever, when he questioned us at length about our
masturbatory habits as gravely as if he were the Masters
and Johnson of American letters. One seldom resisted such
an unabashed craving for all the news of human life. I don't
suggest that such memories constitute revelations. Jim
Dickey's middle years were lived not in an unlit corner but
on the small yet feverishly observed stage that academics
and other famished readers reserve for the Great Man In
(and, only lately, the Great and equally Reckless Woman).
Most of the people whom Jim's debauches troubled were
adults who had after all volunteered with open eyes to
stand in his path. Nevertheless, their regrets and cold but
live outrage remain a large and troublesome part of what
the name Dickey now connotes. Only a few weeks before
his death, I tried to nominate Jim for an important poetry
prize only to discover that my colleagues on the commit-
tee — all eminent writers and critics — were still in various states of rejection; and it seemed to me likely that
their aversion was occasioned more by the memory or
rumor of Dickey Berserk than by extensive knowledge of
the imposing quantity of unassailable work he produced
till the end.

My own final memory is a good deal more spacious and
complicated. In the summer of 1994, Jim and I were invited
to London to participate in a British festival of "Southern
Culture." He and I, several other writers, B. B. King and

numerous young bluesmen, dancers, storytellers, and the world's greatest collector of Elvis memorabilia (whose collection included three actual Presley body parts) were bedded at the same small hotel for 10 days of highly uncharacteristic and un-air-conditioned London swelter. Each morning when I'd come down for breakfast at 8, Jim would already be seated in the lounge, drinking his first double whisky of the day. I'd invite him to join me for bacon and eggs; he'd wave me on but invite me to stop on my way back. So for a week of mornings, and as many midnights, I would sit alone with Jim and hear his late thoughts.

His health was dire, his domestic situation tragic; but he said he was working every day to "press it all out." By "it" he plainly meant the poetry left in him; and though I silently wondered if so battered a frame could bear such pressure, he revealed in a masterly and entirely unapologetic reading on the last night of the festival that potent work still ran down his long arms and through his huge fingers. When we parted the next day (we'd never meet again), he brought me a photograph of himself sitting at the actual desk of Edgar Allan Poe with a stuffed raven on his shoulder. We both laughed. But I'm left here now with the surety that a substantial part of James Dickey's work will, like the equally anguished Poe's, outlast his sad life — no embalmed black bird but a stalwart live hawk loved by the sun.

Allen Ginsberg
1926–1997

by

DIANE DI PRIMA

I MET ALLEN GINSBERG'S WORK a few months before I
met Allen himself. Soon after "Howl" came out in 1956,
a friend came to dinner in my Hell's Kitchen apartment
in Manhattan and brought me a copy. I was moved and
delighted. For several years, I had been writing poetry and
stories in the "hip" argot of the period — much to the horror of everyone I knew — and now, here it was. Language
I loved had broken into print. I felt strong and vindicated.

It's probably hard for anyone now to realize just how
much that book meant to us writers and artists who were
in our early 20s back then. It was a difficult time. We had
all had our Carl Solomons. Some friend locked away in
prison or madhouse or worse, dead or disabled from electric shock. There was no one in my generation who didn't
carry some such tale in mind and heart, so Allen immediately and at once spoke for all of us. It was his special gift.
If artists are "the antennae of the race," then poets are
articulate antennae, and Allen throughout his life had a
particular knack for speaking the concerns that were as
yet only on the periphery of consciousness.

I was just 22 and I acted with the quickness of that age.

I wrote to Ginsberg in care of City Lights Books in San Francisco, and I sent some work. Not to publish especially, just to share something with like-minded folk. I got an encouraging letter from Lawrence Ferlinghetti almost immediately and a few months later Ginsberg himself appeared at my door. He arrived unannounced (we had no phone in any case) and stayed for a couple of days. He brought several friends with him, including his lover, Peter Orlovsky, and Jack Kerouac. They were all on their way to Europe and Morocco.

Many things transpired in the short time that they were in my house, but suffice it to say that betwixt and between satisfying various voracious and youthful appetites, we talked writing and read our work to each other, morning, noon and night. It was a great feast of the word.

*   *
*

On summer solstice in 1968, I moved to the West Coast to be closer to my Zen teacher, Shunryu Suzuki, and to work with the Diggers and others on the social and economic changes we deemed to be not only possible but imminent. I've been there ever since.

A couple of years later, Allen called to invite me to Boulder to teach at the first summer session of what was to become Naropa Institute and, over the next 22 years, I spent a part of many summers at Naropa. It became a gathering place for the tribe of writers to which I belonged. We would go to Boulder, teach for a week or two and catch up on each other's lives and thought, and I remember returning home one night, a few years back, to the student housing where we lived. Allen and I were let out of someone's car at his corner and began our way up the stairs. I distinctly remember the balmy feel of the air, the street lights through the green leaves and the brown color of the building. Allen, his hand on a thin metal banister, paused mid-step, his foot in the air, smiled his wry sad smile that gently laughed at himself and whomever he was talking to and said with just a touch of astonishment: "We are growing old in this place."

This past summer, I taught at Naropa for the entire month of the summer program, partly to hang out with Allen and my other poet-friends, while I finished working on my long poem, "Loba," for Viking Press. The first night, we were all thrown into panic when Allen was taken to a Boulder hospital with what everyone thought was a heart attack. It was finally determined that he was suffering from altitude sickness and exhaustion, but this event, coming as it did at the start of the summer term, colored everything after. Allen went to innumerable readings and other poets' classes, as he always had, but I think we were all aware that he looked very thin and frail.

By fall, Allen seemed better. He and I played the DNA Lounge, a club south of Market Street here in San Francisco. The reading was a benefit for Pema Osel Ling, a practitioner and fellow poet. Peter called from Los Angeles. The prognosis, Peter told me, was one to three months. I called Allen's office in New York the next morning. I was flying east in a couple of days to do some teaching "on the road" and thought to stop in New York when I was done to say goodbye to my old friend. Both Allen and I, I knew, had been Buddhist long enough to have a matter-of-fact attitude about our deaths.

I got Bob Rosenthal, Allen's longtime secretary, and

he suggested I call just before coming down: Allen was expected home in a day or so, the staff was arranging for hospice care and he hoped everything would be in place and a visit would be possible. He said he was worried about how many people would want to visit and how to handle the whole thing. Would I please not tell anyone the news for a day or two, so Allen could get settled in before there was an influx of questions and folks from the news media? Of course, he added with a touch of resignation, that Allen had been on the phone at the hospital all day long. I promised not to put the word out. . . .

The same evening, April 1, around 8:30 San Francisco time, I got a call from Allen. He told me he was dying and sounded calm and interested. He spoke more slowly than usual but in a steady stream and, as always, it was hard to get a word in. He thought he might have a few weeks and he had plenty of plans. His plan was to rent a grand piano and put it in his new loft. So that people could come and make music with him. He had a contract for three records and, though he had plenty of material, he was full of new ideas. He had been feeling ill, he said, for about four months and during that time, he had written a whole now book of poems. He was especially excited about a poem describing his fantasies of his funeral. "I realized," he told me, "that everyone fantasizes about their funeral, and it was a terrific thing to write about. It's a very funny poem."

We talked for about half an hour. Allen was pleased that he had gotten all his affairs in order; he would go out with no loose ends. For Naropa Institute, ever dear to his heart, he had arranged a large contribution from a philanthropist friend. "When you're dying," he told me with a chuckle, "you can ask for anything." We agreed I'd come down and see him on April 14. "Call Bob," he told me. "We can always find a half hour."

On April 3, Allen slipped into a coma. His Buddhist teacher, Gelek Rinpoche, flew out to be with him. He died at 2:39 a.m. on April 5.

I got the call about 11 in Syracuse, N.Y., a staging point on the journey to my poetry gig. It was just a few months more than 40 years since he had burst with Kerouac into my cold-water flat in Hell's Kitchen. It will take awhile to really know he's gone.

"What has the world lost?" a public radio announcer asked me, a few days later. "Nothing," I told him. "There are the things Allen didn't get to do, the poems he didn't write. But he didn't write them. You can't lose what you never had."

I wish it were true.

William S. Burroughs

1914–1997

by

RICHARD SEAVER

So WILLIAM BURROUGHS too has passed into the night, a realm he knew intimately alive and will doubtlessly master dead. For Bill, through most of his 83 years, was more attuned to and focused on a world beyond the so-called normal than he was to the mundane matters we associate with daily living. He was truly, consistently and completely a rebel, a maverick, a freewheeling original who abhorred boundaries and any kind of restriction, social or artistic, and especially governmental. Throughout his life, he harbored a hatred of sham, hypocrisy, the cowardice of conformism, be it familial, peer or social — whatever could cause you to deviate from or compromise your true self. Diogenes with a knife and a gun.

Not to canonize the man: As a youth, he was in constant trouble. He wrecked the family car, got tossed out of schools, drank, was reclusive and moody. As the grandson of the inventor of the adding machine, William Seward Burroughs II, he was proudly named after his grandfather: by rights he should have been a millionaire. Fortunately, largely because his grandfather was as poor as a businessman as he was clever as an inventor, his watered-down "fortune" gave Bill a small monthly pension, just enough to give him the freedom to do what he wanted provided poverty was not a deterrent.

For Burroughs — introverted, homosexual, depressive, junky — writing became his refuge. In the silence of his room, often a spare, rundown hotel room in a remote part of the globe, he could close the door to people and the world and create his own characters, his own time-space continuum.

Roughly the first half of his life was a constant, restless exploration of the flawed self; from the 1950s on, an uncompromising acid evaluation of the more than flawed landscape of the second half of the 20th century. He lived in half a dozen countries, from Mexico to Colombia to France to Morocco, experimenting with drugs, living in an underworld of homosexuality and trafficking, in the largest sense of the term. His lifestyle of willful alienation, and his laser mind, increasingly attracted younger iconoclasts and "misfits" to him and, although he still had published nothing, he was at 40 fast becoming the guru of what would become known as the Beat Generation.

His masterful biographer, Ted Morgan, named him and titled his work "Literary Outlaw," which was both apt and accurate. His fellow writer and fellow junky, Alex Trocchi, my closest friend for many years, once described himself as a "cosmonaut of inner space," a description that fit Burroughs far more than it did Trocchi. Just before he turned 40, Burroughs finally published in 1953 his first novel, *Junky*, thanks to the efforts of Allen Ginsberg, who idolized him. Like most first novels, especially the new and different, *Junky*, an original paperback, was completely neglected.

Not a single review. But at least he was a published author.

I met Burroughs in the spring of 1961, in Paris, at the dubious but sumptuous headquarters of one Maurice Girodias, another rebel, the founder-owner of Olympia Press, who had made a small fortune publishing Vladimir Nabokov's *Lolita* and was squandering the proceeds as quickly as possible by opening a restaurant on the Left Bank, La Grande Séverine, the cellar of which was a tango-oriented Latin-band nightclub.

I was working for Grove Press, which had recently contracted with Burroughs to be the American publisher of *Naked Lunch*, and Grove owner Barney Rosset and I, who was to be his editor, were there to meet the man. Having read *Naked Lunch*, I was not sure what to expect but whatever my mind's eye had conjured up bore no resemblance to the real thing. Girodias and (I presumed) Burroughs were seated at a table at La Grande Séverine, hardly speaking. Could this shy and distinguished-looking, bespectacled, neatly dressed gentleman, with his gaunt face and misty eyes, be the redoubtable author of the revolutionary novel? He looked more like a banker, or maybe an undertaker, than like a rebel with a cause. Polite to a fault, he seemed to me remote and withdrawn.

But as lunch progressed, and the wine flowed, he loosened up and began to talk about the genesis of the book: how and when he had written it over a long period and how the monstrous manuscript had been shaped and pared by his two Paris friends, Brion Gysin and Sinclair Belies. It had come out in France in a first printing of 10,000 copies, considerably more than the usual Olympia printing, and had been duly banned, as were all Olympia titles. But the desultory censors, who took six months to read and ban the book, gave readers time enough to snap up the first edition.

We explained to Burroughs that the climate in America was inauspicious, and we outlined our plan to change it. *Lady Chatterley's Lover* had been published, had been the subject of countless lawsuits but had finally prevailed in a federal court decision. Next was Henry Miller's *Tropic of Cancer* due out that year. Then would come *Naked Lunch.*

He listened quietly, said he understood completely and indicated he would do whatever was needed to ensure American publication, adding, "providing I don't have to promote the book personally in any way." Personal promotion was much less prevalent than it is today, and we assured Burroughs that that would not be a problem. The parting was cordial, if formal. I left still puzzled, wondering if the man I had met was the real Bill Burroughs, author of some of the wildest, most innovative prose I had ever read.

Over the next 25 years, I edited eight more of Burroughs' prose works in three incarnations: at Grove; at Seaver Books, a 1970s imprint of Viking; and at Henry Holt. We had a set pattern for preparing a manuscript. Burroughs would send in a new work only when he felt it was ready for press. "I would welcome your comments as usual," he wrote at one point, "but I feel the manuscript is now as I want it." I would read it, comment on it in detail and send it back. Then we would set up a time to meet, almost always in New York, where we would spend a full two or three days going through the manuscript page by page. The normal process.

But unlike so many other authors, Burroughs, who knew

precisely what he wanted, never argued or lost his cool. If we disagreed, he would patiently explain the reason and background for a certain scene, a phrase, description, dialogue. Yes, dialogue: To make his point on this score, his wont was to read aloud the questioned passage, in his Midwestern twang, his voice altering from character to character unerringly.

His dour exterior belied the depth and extent of his humor, for Burroughs' satire is scathing and his humor dark as pitch. I find him to be one of the truly funniest writers of our time. And his dialogues, especially read by him, are hilarious. (I only hope, before he departed, that his devoted followers found time to have Bill record key passages of his opus for future generations.) Scandalous, too. Burroughs was one of the rare writers who knew, by the nature of his subjects, by the unsparing rawness of his prose and by the complex, demanding nature of his novelistic structure, that he was doubtless condemning himself to commercial failure. We talked about this a lot, and though I never suggested toning anything down, I did tell him on several occasions that I doubted he could hope — at least in his lifetime — to reach a wide audience. "Later wouldn't be bad," he once murmured.

But the relative lack of commercial success never really seemed to rankle him. I told him, citing Beckett, whom he had met, that I was confident that in the long run he would prevail after the critics and erudites had done their digging and the world had caught up. And I believe Bill believed that, too. *Cities of the Red Night*, the last book I edited with him, enjoyed perhaps the greatest critical success since *Naked Lunch* and sold 20,000 hardcover copies, a respectable sale. It wasn't mega, but the curve was upward.

At his 75th birthday party, he was in fine fettle, feted by young and old alike, the old guard protective, the young kowtowing to the impassive master. I looked at him with awe, at the Buster Keaton face beneath which lurked (I felt) an urge to roar with laughter; age had made its inroads, but he looked so very much like the man I had met almost 30 years before.

When he hit the tarmac of 80, not necessarily running but still shooting and creating (if essentially in graphic form now rather than in prose), I marveled at the tough inner core. God, he'd abused his body. No: used it in an endless harsh experiment: Anyway, looking at him, I figured he'd outlive us all. Then, when I heard the news, it occurred to me why he decided to go: With Jack and Gregory and Brion and so many others, and now Allen, already there paving the way, what the hell, it was high time for him to "join the room of the ruined warehouse swept by winds of time. . . ."

Martha Gellhorn

1908–1998

by

BILL BUFORD

M Y DEAR WILLIAM. Note: That's William. Not Bill. You must change your name. No one will ever take you seriously. Bill Buford? No, it just won't do. And your hair. You've got to do something with your hair. And that beard — shave it. You look like Allen Ginsberg." I'm quoting Martha Gellhorn, the novelist and war reporter who died last Monday, and whose work I had the privilege of publishing for much of her last decade, her ninth.

"I forgot to add, William, you must buy new trousers that don't look like what the well-dressed young elephants are wearing this year. How else can you win the Iranian's love?" The Iranian in question was a particularly elusive girlfriend. Martha tutored me on matters of the heart, and on drinking (you could never drink enough), and on my appearance (a disaster) and on my manners — especially my manners: My manners, in Martha's eyes, were catastrophic. "I'll be in London for a few days later this month," she wrote me after we had a little row arising from another one of my behavioral misdemeanors, and the exchange must have become so rude and abusive that — and I infer this from the correspondence that I'm rereading for the first time — I sunk into a sulk. "If you don't return my call, I'll sadly take it that you wish to sever relations forever. A pity. But think about it, William. I may be the only old person you know, and elders and betters are necessary, as I know with despair, now that all of mine are dead."

The elementary facts of her life. Born nearly 90 years ago. Bossy, straight-talking, cigarette-smoking. The boozy reporter of wars and of the plight of the down-and-out. Also a writer of short stories, novellas and novels. And a travel writer. She was married to Ernest Hemingway, and she hated the fact that, whenever her work was written about in the press, his name was invariably mentioned as well, just as I'm mentioning it.

But it's hard to avoid: The two of them met when the world was at its most dramatic. They fell in love at the outbreak of the Spanish Civil War and divorced once World War II had ended, and in between were Cuba and big-game hunting and trips to China and battlefields in Finland and Barcelona and the beaches of Normandy. Could there be any two people more romantic? He was Papa Hemingway by then and she was — what? Blond and thin and sassy, a starlet of the highest order, a young Lauren Bacall, except that she was prettier and sexier and a whole lot brainier than a young Lauren Bacall. There was a glamour about Martha Gellhorn, the glamour of black-and-white movies. It was in her manner and her way with the ways of the world. She was a dame.

Seventeen years ago, I hadn't read Martha Gellhorn, but I was editing a literary magazine and putting together an issue of travel writing and someone said I should ask her to contribute. A piece about a journey to Haiti was the result — dramatic and eventful (a white woman on an island of angry blacks who nearly gets stoned) and full of what I would come to recognize as Gellhorn rage — the irrepressible, passionate rage against injustice. "The Big Picture always exists," she wrote, and by Big Picture she meant the drama of power brokers and politicians and corporations. "And I seem to have spent my life observing how desperately the Big Picture affects the little people who did not devise it and have no control over it."

Why was I discovering her only now? I learned later that Penguin had brought out her first book in years, *Travels With Myself and Another* (that reluctant "another" was of course the famous writer who will remain nameless), but the experience was not a happy one for either author or publisher, and the book's initial sales were modest. But I was so excited to have come upon her — this American in Britain, this throwback to a time when truth was truth and right was right and wrong was an identifiable thing that must be fought at all costs — that I fell for her. I wanted to do everything for her. I wanted to publish her in my magazine. I wanted to publish her books. I wanted to be her agent. I wanted to see her work translated, brought back into print, made into movies. And for a brief period (both of us fools), she let me be all these things: editor, publisher, agent — the works. But I was still in my 20s and believed that there was nothing I couldn't do, and she, nearly 50 years older, probably should have known better.

Her letters to me are postmarked Belize and Kenya and Tanzania and the south of Spain — she was happiest in places where she could wear little — but her home was a cottage in the Welsh countryside, where she drank booze, read mystery novels and wrote until she got tired of her

company and came into London, where she had a flat on
Cadogan Square. Her days there were tightly organized —
drinks and dinners and maybe a nightcap. She didn't have
parties — she rarely saw people in groups — but met with
her friends, one by one: John Pilger, Paul Theroux, James
Fox, Nicholas Shakespeare, John Hatt, Jeremy Harding.
Those were some of her regular men friends. We'd see each
other — one of us on the way out, while another was arriv-
ing. She had some women friends, but Martha liked men,
was easy around them and could be flirty and coquettish
even at the age of 85. She was, she once recalled, thrown off
a press boat on the Normandy invasion (Hemingway with
whom she was by then in a relation of unmitigated acri-
mony, had taken her credentials) and summarily returned
to Britain. But then, by her own account, she flirted her
way back onto another boat (a hospital ship) and, stowed
away in a toilet, made the crossing and saw the invasion
firsthand. It was a telling incident, unintimidated by one of
the most dangerous military operations of the war (and so
fearless in a male way), and yet utterly capable of making
men melt (devastating in a distinctly female way). And of
course Hemingway.

I brought him up the first time I went to her flat for dinner. It was the forbidden subject. "William," she said, "I
have only one response to people when they bring up that
name. And that's to show them the door." She didn't show
me the door. In fact, the taboo having been broken, she
went on to talk about him at great length — both that
evening and on many occasions thereafter. My speculation
is that, in fact, he was the important man in her life. Yes,
she resented him, loathed being seen not as an author in
her own right but as the difficult adjunct to the famous

man of American letters. But he was the only man she talked about.

Sometimes it was Ernest the monster (how he terrified his children) and sometimes Ernest the myth (he was, in her words, "shy in bed," and had, she was convinced, slept with no more than five women). She was fed up with him by the end of World War II — he'd grown lazy and bloated and indifferent to history — but she had respect for the writing. She talked about the philosophy of his sentences and the business of paring them back until they were as direct and true as they could possibly be — something she did herself in her own tough, often staccato prose. She said many, many more things — vivid and indiscreet at the time — but usually uttered under the influence of her liquor cabinet or the bottles of wine that we'd have at dinner ("tight as a tick" was one of her phrases), and few details now remain. Once I recall writing something down on a napkin — Martha had gone to the loo, having just revealed something wonderfully salacious — but I was so drunk that I later blew my nose into it and then threw it away.

There was a growing suspicion among Martha's friends that she would never die. There was too much energy, too much determination to be curtailed by something as ordinary as mortality. She had a 90th birthday coming up in November. Surely she'd make that. And there was the prospect of another war in Iraq (she was in a rage about even the Friday before her death) — pure Gellhorn. She wouldn't allow herself to miss that. But she will. And she did.

I feel so lucky to have known her, this proof of the human spirit, the naysayer to naysayers. I know her friends do too. Now we just have her books.

Andre Dubus

1936–1999

by

FREDERICK BUSCH

I'VE ALWAYS THOUGHT OF ANDRE as a religious writer. I believe that he actively worshipped his Lord as Roman Catholics require of themselves that they do, and I know that even his toughest, most seemingly earthbound work had to do with the relationship, as he understood it, between humanity and (as he understood it) heaven. Andre carried his God within him, and, for more secular urgencies, a shotgun and an axe handle in the trunk of his car.

He wrote about crusty Marines and beat-up, downtrodden children, and girls whose womanhood did not beckon with promise; and he wrote of men and women whose lives were so far past the promise they once had wished to see that they were, although not old, already looking back. And he wrote these stories of difficult lives with a prose so graceful, so intent on achieving the beauty he believed, he swore, he wished, and maybe even knew was within them, that their dark lives flickered, a little, with the light of his sure, unsentimental language.

He came to Colgate University in the '80s, with Peggy and their infant child — she was breastfed in the back of the room while Andre answered questions up front — and later they napped, all three of them in our living room. Their ribs rose and fell, it seemed, in unison in the autumn sun that gathered in the house. It was a portrait of plenty, of ease, a fine moment of fullness. And that night Andre read, for what he said was the first time, "A Father's Story" We were in a large room at Colgate, and it was packed. He was pleased but also apprehensive, I thought; so I knew the story mattered to him, for, while he always treated his work and his audience with respect, he was almost worried that night. I believe he suspected that the story was large: that he had woven a seine very well, and he had caught a great creature.

The story is, of course, large and living. It walks the dangerous edge of emotion — his work dares to go there, risking (as we should) sentimentality in order to explore feeling. And it looks directly at, talks directly to Andre's God and his profound sense of the immensity involved in fathering. It is a great story, and we all, that night, knew it. One after another, once the silence of expelled breath — we had been struck a blow: he worked physically as well as metaphysically — followed his ending, and once we had taken a breath, I heard sobbing. It came not from one of the more than a hundred people in the room; it came from many singly and in clusters, the college women in the audience came forward to tell him of their love for their own father.

"My father would have done that," a student told him between sobs referring to the fictive father's willingness to break the law to save his daughter, risking cosmic as well as earthly punishment to emulate his Lord.

"Of course he would have, darlin'," Andre said, "and you should go out here — I saw a pay phone out there in the hall — and you call him up and tell him you love him."

One by one — I followed to see — they called, as their turn came, and they told their father of the story they'd been read. And then they passed along the message of love they had found in the story.

I do not think he meant to be telling his readers how to live. And he would have bridled at my use of "message," as — even while saying it — I do, too. Andre Dubus did not write scripture lessons or any other kind of lessons. He wrote about the soul in its agonies and occasional triumphs, and he pushed the language — with respect — as hard as he could. He tried to make beauty. And he succeeded. And now he is in our stories. Because of him, they're good ones. But, because he died from us they all — in spite of the abiding art he left us — end unhappily.

Eudora Welty

1909–2001

by

JONATHAN YARDLEY

In the spring of 1973, I spent about a week in Jackson, much of it in the company of the Mississippi capital's most famous resident, Eudora Welty. I soon discovered that she was an ardent devotee of the NBC evening news. Late one afternoon I suggested that it was time to shut down the tape recorder. "Oh, let's do," she said. "We've got to go and hear the Watergate!" When I teased her about this, she described watching the news one evening a few years earlier while signing copies of her books. She glanced down and realized that she had signed several "David Brinkley."

It was commonly assumed that Eudora, whose stories and novels often have a magical, ethereal quality, was herself otherworldly, but quite the opposite was true. She was fiercely interested in politics and public affairs, and had pungent opinions. "I'm a Democrat," she told me, "and I suppose I'm fairly liberal, but that doesn't mean I go along with the party line every time." She loathed Richard Nixon — "Nothing could make me vote for Nixon; I've never voted for him" — but she was irate about George McGovern's campaign against him in 1972: "That was the most abysmal presidential campaign we've ever had. It was the one time I've never voted. It was so dispiriting."

She rarely ventured to Washington, but she kept a weather eye on it. A particular friend of hers was Jim Lehrer, the public-television newsman and moderator of presidential debates, to whom she was devoted not merely because of his exemplary personal qualities but also because he made her feel connected to public as well as private matters. But in the end it was the latter in which she was most passionately interested, so by way of paying tribute to her at the end of her long, incredibly fruitful life — she died last week in Jackson at the age of 92 — I would like to say a few words about her keen understanding of the crucial differences between what the novelist does and what the political or ideological "crusader" does.

In the late 1950s and early 1960s, as Mississippi became the battleground of the civil rights struggle, Eudora came under heavy pressure from outside to speak up on behalf of the black activists and their white allies. Eudora had been ardently supportive of their cause all her life, and well before the 1950s had treated black characters in her fiction with respect and sympathy, but she declined to mount the pulpit. Instead, in 1961 she published an essay in the *Atlantic Monthly* called "Must the Novelist Crusade?" It is an extraordinary document, not merely the definitive explanation of how "writing fiction places the novelist and the crusader on opposite sides" but also a window into one of the sharpest, most discriminating minds that American literature has known.

Pleas that she turn her fiction into an expression of her political views, Eudora wrote, arose from "an honest and understandable zeal to allot every writer his chance to better the world or go to his grave reproached for the mess it is in," but failed to comprehend the essential task of the writer of fiction, which is not to "argue," but "to show, to disclose." Here are a few extracts from her line of reasoning:

We cannot in fiction set people to acting mechanically or carrying placards to make their sentiments plain. People are not Right and Wrong, Good and Bad, Black and White personified; flesh and blood and the sense of comedy object. . . . The novelist works neither to correct nor to condone, not at all to comfort, but to make what's told alive. He assumes at the start an enlightenment in his reader equal to his own, for they are hopefully on the point of taking off together from that base into the rather different world of the imagination. . . .

Writing fiction is an interior affair. Novels and stories always will be put down little by little out of personal feeling and personal beliefs arrived at alone and at firsthand over a period of time as time is needed. To go outside and beat the drum is only to interrupt, interrupt, and so finally to forget and to lose. Fiction has, and must keep, a private address. . . .

Indifference would indeed be corrupting to the fiction writer, indifference to any part of man's plight. Passion is the chief ingredient of good fiction. It flames right out of sympathy for the human condition and goes into all great writing. . . . But to distort a work of passion for the sake of a cause is to cheat, and the end, far from justifying the means, is fairly sure to be lost with it.

It is difficult to imagine a more eloquent or lucid argument against the exploitation of fiction for political or ideological ends, or for that matter against the use of art in any form for such ends. Those words were written as the country's writers and artists were beginning to take up political arms for the first time since the 1930s, and no doubt they will seem antediluvian to many readers today, accustomed as we have become since 1961 to soapbox novelists such as Don DeLillo, John Updike, Toni Morrison and Philip Roth. Yet they draw, with absolute clarity, the line between "the novel and the editorial," which as Eudora said are "equally valid" but — and this is what matters — wholly different.

Among many other things, "Must the Novelist Crusade?" reminds us that in addition to being a novelist and story writer of the first rank, Eudora was a superbly gifted essayist. Her mind was as orderly as it was creative, which permitted her to see the world and its inhabitants with as much precision as love. She was, quite simply, a wonder.

Saul Bellow
1915–2005

BY

JAMES WOOD

I JUDGED ALL modern prose by his. Unfair, certainly, because he made even the fleet-footed — the Updikes, the DeLillos, the Roths — seem like monopodes. Yet what else could I do? I discovered Saul Bellow's prose in my late teens, and henceforth, the relationship had the quality of a love affair about which one could not keep silent. Over the last week, much has been said about Bellow's prose, and most of the praise — perhaps because it has been overwhelmingly by men — has tended toward the robust: We hear about Bellow's mixing of high and low registers, his Melvillean cadences jostling the jivey Yiddish rhythms, the great teeming democracy of the big novels, the crooks and frauds and intellectuals who loudly people the brilliant sensorium of the fiction. All of this is true enough; John Cheever, in his journals, lamented that, alongside Bellow's fiction, his stories seemed like mere suburban splinters. Ian McEwan wisely suggested last week that British writers and critics may have been attracted to Bellow precisely because he kept alive a Dickensian amplitude now lacking in the English novel.

But nobody mentioned the beauty of this writing, its music, its high lyricism, its firm but luxurious pleasure in language itself. Like all serious novelists, Bellow read poetry: Shakespeare first (he could recite lines and lines from the plays, remembered from his school days in Chicago), then Milton, Keats, Wordsworth, Hardy, Larkin, and his old friend John Berryman. And, behind all this, with its English stretching all the way back into deeper antiquity, the King James Bible. Nobody mentioned the way Bellow could describe a river as "crimped, green, blackish, glassy," or Chicago as "blue with winter, brown with evening, crystal with frost," or New York as "sheer walls, gray spaces, dry lagoons of tar and pebbles." Here is a paragraph, one of my favorite in all Bellow, from the story "The Old System":

On the airport bus, he opened his father's copy of the Psalms. The black Hebrew letters only gaped at him like open mouths with tongues hanging down, pointing upward, flaming but dumb. He tried — forcing. It did no good. The tunnel, the swamps, the auto skeletons, machine entrails, dumps, gulls, sketchy Newark trembling in fiery summer, held his attention minutely. . . . Then in the plane running with concentrated fury to take off — the power to pull away from the magnetic earth, and more: When he saw the ground tilt backward, the machine rising from the runway, he said to himself in clear internal words, "Shema Yisroel," Hear, O Israel, God alone is God! On the right, New York leaned gigantically seaward, and the plane with a jolt of retracted wheels turned toward the river. The Hudson green within green, and rough with tide and wind. Isaac released the breath he had been holding, but sat belted tight. Above the marvelous bridges, over clouds, sailing in atmosphere, you know better than ever that you are no angel.

I suppose there must be people — as there are people left cold by Mozart or Brahms — who are untouched by such a passage, though I pity them. Bellow had a habit of writing repeatedly about flying, partly, I used to think, because it was the great obvious advantage he had over his dead competitors, those writers who had never seen the world from above the clouds: Melville, Tolstoy, Proust. And how well he does it! In sentence after sentence the world is captured with brimming novelty: Newark seen as "sketchy" and "trembling in fiery summer"; the jet "running with concentrated fury to take off" (a phrase that, with its unpunctuated onrush, itself enacts such a concentrated fury); New York, which, as the plane tilts, "leaned gigantically seaward" (say the phrase to yourself, and see how the words themselves — "leaned gi-gan-tic-ally sea-ward" — elongate the experience so that the very language embodies the queasiness it describes); the dainty, unexpected rhythm of "The Hudson green within green, and rough with tide and wind" ("green within green" captures very precisely the different shades of green that we see in water when several thousand feet above it); and finally, "sailing in atmosphere" — isn't that exactly what the freedom of flight feels like? And yet, until this moment, one did not have these words — the best words, the right words in the right order — to fit this feeling. Until this moment, one was comparatively inarticulate; until this moment, one had been blandly inhabiting a deprived eloquence.

How, exactly, does one thank a writer for this? Fifteen years ago, at the age of twenty-four, when I was working for *The Guardian* in London, I did so the only way I knew how: I arranged to meet Bellow and interviewed him for that newspaper. Over the years, I wrote about him again and again and visited him whenever I could. By happy accident, I co-taught a class with him at Boston University. My daughter played with his; our family became close to Bellow and his wife Janis, and to his devoted assistant, Will. I accompanied him on the piano when he played the recorder. It was a delight to talk to him about literature, to make him laugh — he would throw his head back and give out a distinctive chortle, "ha, ha, ha, ha," each laugh separately articulated — and to laugh with him when he was making a joke.

But I cannot say that I truly knew him (partly because I knew him only in his old age); and, in some ways, the human distance was of my making, not his, for my literary gratitude was literally unspeakable, and floated massively above us. The prose was what I truly knew before I knew the man, and always I felt magically indebted in his presence. Like anyone, writers, of course, are embarrassed by excessive praise, just as readers are burdened by their excessive gratitude — one cannot keep going on about it. And, eventually, it is easier to turn the beloved literary work into a kind of disembodied third party: to admit that the work itself exceeds the writer, that it sails — sails in atmosphere, indeed! — away from the writer and toward the delighted reader. In the final year of Saul's life, as he became very frail, I would read some of his own prose to him; something he would doubtless have found, as a younger man, mawkish or cloying or tiresome. It did not feel any of those things, as Bellow sat there in forgetful frailty; rather it felt as if I were gently reminding him of his own talent and that he was grateful for this, and perhaps grateful for my gratitude. But, in truth, I could not thank him enough when he was alive, and I cannot now.

BIOGRAPHIES

EDWARD ABBEY (1927–1989) The Pennsylvania-born writer and environmentalist discovered the Southwest when he entered the University of New Mexico in 1947. He never left. Besides such novels as *The Monkey Wrench Gang* (1975) and *Hayduke Lives* (1989), he is remembered for his essays and *Desert Solitaire* (1968), a classic of environmental literature.

SHERWOOD ANDERSON (1876–1941) Born into small-town life in Ohio, the novelist and short-story writer would immortalize the lives of small-town people in *Winesburg, Ohio* (1919), his best known book. His finest short stories appear in *The Triumph of the Egg* (1921) and *Horses and Men* (1923).

JAMES BALDWIN (1924–1987) Raised in New York City's Harlem, Baldwin was heralded as a literary successor to Richard Wright with the publication of his first novel, *Go Tell It on the Mountain* (1953). Most of his subsequent novels dealt with race and social problems. He is also considered a powerful and important American essayist.

SAUL BELLOW (1915–2005) The Chicago-based novelist won all the big prizes: three National Book Awards, the Pulitzer Prize, and, in 1976, the Nobel Prize in literature. He published ten full-length novels, two of which, *The Adventures of Augie March* (1954) and *Henderson the Rain King* (1959), appeared on the Modern Library's list of the 100 best novels published in the English language in the twentieth century.

TED BERRIGAN (1934–1983) Born and raised in Providence, Rhode Island, Berrigan moved to New York in the early 1960s and became a central figure in the second generation of the New York School of Poets which included Anselm Hollo, Ron Padgett, and Anne Waldman. He wrote over more than twenty books.

BILL BUFORD (b. 1954) The American editor and writer attended King's College, Cambridge, and remained in England after graduation where he became editor of the British literary quarterly *Granta*. He is also the author of *Among the Thugs* (1992). Upon returning to the United States he became literary editor of the *New Yorker*.

WILLIAM S. BURROUGHS (1914–1997) Considered a major force in twentieth-century literature, Burroughs lived a semi-legendary life between Paris, London, and Tangiers, writing a series of boldly experimental novels, with themes of addiction, homosexuality, and war. They include *Naked Lunch* (1959) and *The Soft Machine* (1961).

FREDERICK BUSCH (1941–2006) A long-time professor of English at Colgate University, Busch was the author of more than two dozen books, including novels, short-story collections, essays, and literary criticism.

WENDY CAMPBELL (b. 1939) Campbell was a friend of Sylvia Plath and Ted Hughes while they were all attending Cambridge University.

HENRY SEIDEL CANBY (1878–1961) A critic and editor, Canby earned a Ph.D. from Yale in 1899 and later founded *The Yale Review*. His *The Short Story in English* (1908) was a standard text on the subject for many years, and his biographical studies of Thoreau, Henry James, and Mark Twain remain useful works.

WILLA CATHER (1876–1947) Associated with the state of Nebraska where she grew up, Cather was a journalist before she produced her famous novels *O Pioneers!* (1913) and *My Ántonia* (1918). Her travels and interest in the Southwest inspired her novel of colonial New Mexico, *Death Comes for the Archbishop* (1937).

JOHN JAY CHAPMAN (1862–1933) The Harvard-educated social commentator, literary critic, dramatist, essayist, and friend of William James used his pen to skewer the get-rich-quick morality of the post–Civil War "Gilded Age."

JOHN CHEEVER (1912–1982) Critic John Leonard dubbed Cheever "our Chekhov of the exurbs" because of his short stories which focused on the lives of New York suburban commuters. They are collected in *The Stories of John Cheever* (1968), which was awarded the Pulitzer Prize. His first novel, *The Wapshot Chronicle* (1957), won the National Book Award.

JOHN CIARDI (1916–1986) The author of more than forty volumes of poetry, Ciardi is probably best known for *How Does a Poem Mean?* (1959), a little book that became a standard text in high school and college English classes. He also served as editor of *Saturday Review* and taught at Harvard and Rutgers.

STEPHEN CRANE (1871–1900) Over the course of his brief life Crane produced a small body of work that has a lasting place in American literature. His short novel *The Red Badge of Courage* (1895) made him famous while still in his mid-twenties. His travels and reporting in Mexico, Cuba, and Europe helped inspire his stories, especially "The Blue Hotel" (1898) and "The Open Boat" (1899).

ROBERT CREELEY (1926–2005) In the 1950s Creeley was part of the faculty of Black Mountain College in North Carolina (along with Charles Olson and Robert Duncan) where he edited the influential *Black Mountain Review*. Through that position and his critical writing he helped nurture a new generation of poets. He published more than sixty books of poetry as well as a dozen of prose.

EDWARD DAHLBERG (1900–1977) A truly original American literary stylist, Dahlberg is best remembered for his remarkable autobiographical books which include *Bottom Dogs* (1930, with an introduction by D. H. Lawrence) and *Because I Was Flesh* (1964).

JONATHAN DANIELS (1902–1981) A friend of Thomas Wolfe at the University of North Carolina, Daniels went on to a career in journalism. Spending time abroad, he completed several novels and, upon returning to the South, wrote on themes often related to the Civil War. After serving in the Roosevelt administration during World War II he wrote a memoir about his Washington experiences.

GUY DAVENPORT (1927–2005) Essayist, poet, translator, and artist, Davenport retired as Distinguished Alumni Professor of English at the University of Kentucky after twenty-seven years in 1991, when he was awarded a MacArthur Fellowship.

JAMES DICKEY (1923–1997) Dickey was awarded the National Book Award in 1965 for his best-known volume of verse, *Buckdancer's Choice*. The following year he was appointed Poetry Consultant to the Library of Congress (an office that subsequently became the Poet Laureate). He was also the author of *Deliverance* (1970), a novel that became a best-seller and a successful motion picture.

DIANE DI PRIMA (b. 1934) Di Prima first became known in the 1950s as part of the Beat movement in New York. She later moved to California, became involved in Buddhism, and raised five children. She now works in San Francisco where she continues to write and teach.

THEODORE DREISER (1871–1945) Like his contemporary Sherwood Anderson, Dreiser grew up in a small town in the Midwest. His novels *Sister Carrie* (1900) and *An American Tragedy* (1925) are often considered to be classics of twentieth-century American fiction.

ANDRE DUBUS (1936–1999) The noted short-story writer and essayist often drew on his personal experiences, from growing up in the South to his confinement to a wheelchair after losing a leg in an accident in 1986. His books include the Pulitzer Prize runner-up *Broken Vessels* (1992) and the National Book Critics Circle Award finalist *Dancing After Hours* (1997).

T. S. ELIOT (1888–1965) Eliot was one of the most distinguished and influential poets of the last century. Though born in St. Louis and educated at Harvard, he moved to London in 1914 and, in 1927, became a British citizen. His poem *The Waste Land* forever changed the landscape of modern poetry. He was awarded the Nobel Prize in Literature in 1948.

RALPH WALDO EMERSON (1803–1882) The essayist and poet was born in Boston where, after finishing Harvard Divinity School, he became a Unitarian minister. The deepening of his philosophical and religious beliefs, along with a trip to Europe where he met Coleridge and Carlyle, made him an independent, non-doctrinal thinker. Moving to nearby Concord, he became the center of the Transcendentalists. His book *Nature* (1836) and his essay "The American Scholar" (1837) are major contributions to American thought.

F. SCOTT FITZGERALD (1896–1940) His first novel, *This Side of Paradise* (1920), published before he was twenty-five, made the author a literary celebrity, and he continued for a decade as a chronicler and notable participant in the "jazz age" of the 1920s. *The Great Gatsby* (1925), written during that era, is a major American novel. Though in creative decline during the next decade, Fitzgerald produced important works, *Tender Is the Night* (1933) and *The Last Tycoon* (1940).

ROBERT FROST (1874–1963) This man of New England was probably the most famous poet of his day, receiving wide public and critical acclaim, America's unofficial laureate. Yet there was a vein of darkness that ran through his work and his life that belied his genial tousled white-haired visage.

MARTHA GELLHORN (1908–1998) Though best known for her groundbreaking journalism, she was also an accomplished fiction writer, author of five novels, fourteen novellas, and two collections of short stories. During her time in Spain she met Hemingway; they married in 1940, he becoming her second husband and she his third wife. The marriage lasted five years, ending when Gellhorn left Hemingway, the only of his wives to do so.

ALLEN GINSBERG (1926–1997) The Newark-born, Columbia-educated poet was a leading figure of the Beat Movement in the 1950s, with his poem *Howl* (1956) becoming, along with Kerouac's *On the Road*, one of its most famous manifestations. He later studied Buddhism and cofounded the Jack Kerouac School of Disembodied Poetics at the Naropa Institute in Boulder, Colorado.

JULIAN HAWTHORNE (1846–1934) The only son of Nathaniel Hawthorne, he enjoyed some success with melodramatic novels, but nothing like the fame of his father. His best works are biographical volumes about his family and the autobiographical *Shapes That Pass* (1928) and *The Memoirs of Julian Hawthorne* (1938).

NATHANIEL HAWTHORNE (1804–1864) A native of Salem, Massachusetts, Hawthorne made an important contribution to early, classic American literature. His frequently symbolic and allegorical treatment of good and evil and sin reflect his New England Puritan background. His novel *The Scarlet Letter* (1850) is an enduring classic of American literature.

ERNEST HEMINGWAY (1899–1961) The famous novelist and short-story writer was born in Illinois, the son of a physician who encouraged a love of the outdoors and hunting, interests that would shape the character and art of the future writer. Hemingway served in

Italy during World War I and was a reporter before and after the war. His first novel, *The Sun Also Rises* (1926), was a success and was followed by *A Farewell to Arms* (1929). Later works include *For Whom the Bell Tolls* (1940) and *The Old Man and the Sea* (1952). In 1952 he was awarded the Nobel Prize. He commited suicide when he was sixty-two.

EDWARD HOAGLAND (b. 1962) Hoagland is one of the finest contemporary American essayists, admired for his award-winning essays exploring the world of nature. He is also the author of novels and a memoir, *Compass Points: How I Lived* (2001).

OLIVER WENDELL HOLMES (1807–1894) While teaching anatomy at Harvard where he received his M.D., Holmes wrote poetry, biography, and novels and became renowned for his witty conversation, much of which was collected in *The Autocrat at the Breakfast Table* (1860) and its successors.

WILLIAM DEAN HOWELLS (1837–1920) A novelist, editor, and critic, Howells grew up in Ohio, became a newspaperman and printer. His early work appeared in the *Atlantic Monthly*, and he was encouraged to move to Boston and pursue a literary career. He worked as a magazine editor for years and produced his important novels, *The Rise of Silas Lapham* (1885) and *A Hazard of New Fortunes* (1890).

ROLFE HUMPHRIES (1894–1969) In addition to being a notable poet, Humphries was a translator, teacher, critic, and editor. Active in the American literary community, he was a vital presence in the life of American poetry in the twenties and thirties.

JAMES GIBBONS HUNEKER (1860–1921) In his role as a journalist in New York, Huneker did much to promote European avant-garde art and music in America during the late nineteenth century. His sharp and colorful criticism was much admired by H. L. Mencken. He also published short stories, a novel, and an autobiography.

HENRY JAMES (1843–1916) Some critics have called James the greatest American novelist of the nineteenth and twentieth centuries. His first writing appeared in American magazines in the 1860s before he embarked to England where he lived most of the remainder of his life. The contrast between the old and the new world is a recurring theme in his work, especially in *Daisy Miller* (1879), *The Portrait of a Lady* (1881), and *The Ambassadors* (1903).

WILLIAM JAMES (1841–1910) The elder brother of Henry James taught at Harvard for thirty-five years and had a special interest in psychology and philosophy. In 1890 he published his classic *Principles of Psychology*. Among his other books are the *Varieties of Religious Experience* (1902) and the exposition of his philosophy, *Pragmatism* (1907).

RANDALL JARRELL (1914–1965) Jarrell established his reputation as a World War II poet. After the war he taught at the Woman's College of the University of North Carolina, Greensboro, and published some of the most admired poetry and literary criticism of his generation.

HUGH KENNER (1923–2003) The Canadian-born critic was at the center of world literature for more than a half-century. Author of many books, he wrote of, and was friends with, such seminal figures of twentieth-century modernism as Samuel Beckett, T. S. Eliot, Ezra Pound, and William Carlos Williams.

RING LARDNER (1885–1933) The newspaperman and short-story writer made his name as a satirist on the publication of *You Know Me, Al* (1916), a series of letters by an imaginary baseball player. Long before the critics discovered Lardner, he had amassed a large popular audience and was one of America's best-known writers during the 1920s.

JOHN LEONARD (b. 1939) Leonard is renowned for his newspaper and magazine television, film, and book reviews and sophisticated observations on contemporary culture. His most recent book is *Lonesome Rangers: Homeless Minds, Promised Lands, Fugitive Cultures* (2002).

DENISE LEVERTOV (1923–1997) In 1947 the English-born poet moved to America and became associated with the Black Mountain group of poets. She later went her own way and became one of the most respected avant-garde poets of her day. During the 1960s her anti-Vietnam War activism infused much of her poetry. She published more than twenty volumes of poetry.

JAMES RUSSELL LOWELL (1819–1891) From a patrician Massachusetts family, Lowell attended Harvard and upon his graduation set off almost immediately on a long career as literary critic and essayist. The first editor of *The Atlantic Monthly*, Lowell is best known for his essays, collected in *Among My Books* (1870) and *My Study Windows* (1871).

ROBERT LOWELL (1917–1977) Born into one of Boston's oldest families, he would become one of the most important American poets of the latter half of the twentieth century. His gifts recognized early on — he received the Pulitzer Prize when he was thirty — his work matured and reached its high point with his collection, *Life Studies* (1959), a watershed work of modern American poetry.

ARCHIBALD MacLEISH (1892–1982) The poet was born in Illinois and educated at Yale. After service in World War I he became part of the American expatriate scene in Paris. He was a friend or acquaintance of virtually an entire generation of American writers, including Pound and Hemingway. He spent several years in public service as Librarian of Congress and later taught at Harvard. His *Collected Poems* (1952) won the Pulitzer Prize and his verse drama, *JB*, was a Broadway success in 1957, earning the author a second Pulitzer.

MARY McCARTHY (1912–1989) Novelist, critic, travel writer, memoirist, Mary McCarthy was always at the center of sophisticated opinion in New York intellectual life. With her companion Philip Rahv she revitalized *Partisan Review*. She later was married to Edmund Wilson. She saw twenty-eight books published during her lifetime.

H. L. MENCKEN (1880–1956) The Baltimore-based newspaperman became nationally known for his editing of the *American Mercury*, a periodical that had an enormous influence on American culture in the 1920s. His literary essays and autobiographical volumes remain interesting reading today.

THOMAS MERTON (1915–1968) The religious writer and poet became a Trappist monk in 1941. His spiritual autobiography, *The Seven Storey Mountain* (1948), was a best-seller. He started publishing first as a poet, then followed with many books on meditation and philosophy.

EDNA ST. VINCENT MILLAY (1892–1950) The Pulitzer Prize-winning poet and playwright was born in Maine, educated at Vassar, and became part of the Greenwich Village and Provincetown bohemian set during the 1920s. Her readings and public appearances made her one of the most famous poets of her era.

TONI MORRISON (b. 1931) The author of, among other novels, *Song of Solomon* (1977) and *Jazz* (1992), Morrison was confirmed as an important American writer with the Pulitzer Prize-winning *Beloved* (1987) which confirmed Morrison as an important American writer. For many years she worked at Random House as an editor while teaching at Princeton. Morrison was awarded the Nobel Prize in literature in 1993.

FLANNERY O'CONNOR (1925–1964) She lived most of her life with her mother on a farm near Milledgeville, Georgia, raising peafowl and writing some of the most distinctive short stories of our time. They were gathered in *The Complete Stories*, which won the 1971 National Book Award.

JOHN O'HARA (1905–1970) O'Hara achieved his first great success with *Appointment in Samarra* (1934). Over the ensuing decades he wrote many short stories for the *New Yorker* and other magazines. As he matured be became well known for long social novels such as *Ten North Frederick* (1955) and *From the Terrace* (1958).

WILLIAM O'ROURKE (b. 1945) The author of four novels and a political columnist for the *Chicago Sun-Times*, O'Rourke is on the Creative Writing faculty of the University of Notre Dame.

SYLVIA PLATH (1932–1963) Born in Boston, she attended Smith College, after which she spent two years at Cambridge University on a Fulbright scholarship, where she met and married poet Ted Hughes and took up permanent residence. After her suicide at age thirty, the poems that were posthumously published established her reputation as a major poet.

KATHERINE ANNE PORTER (1890–1980) The Texas-born writer is much admired for the fine writing style of her short stories. Over a long and tumultuous life, she published little but worked intermittently on a long novel, *Ship of Fools*, which was at last published in 1962 as something of a literary event. Her *Collected Stories* (1965) received both the Pulitzer Prize and the National Book Award.

REYNOLDS PRICE (b. 1933) The North Carolina–born novelist has published more than thirty books and won the National Book Critics Circle Award for his novel *Kate Vaiden* in 1986.

ERNIE PYLE (1900–1944) Probably the best loved and best known war correspondent in American history, Pyle was awarded a Pulitzer Prize in 1944 for his coverage of the World War II military campaigns in Europe. He was with the U. S. forces in the Pacific when he was killed by Japanese machine-gun fire.

PHILIP RAHV (1901–1973) The Russian-born critic and editor was a founder in 1934 of the *Partisan Review* which he helped to maintain as a journal of liberal-to-radical thought in both the literary and social worlds for decades.

MURIEL RUKEYSER (1913–1980) Noted for their social consciousness as well as technical brilliance, Rukeyser's poems cover a wide range of topics and styles. She published twenty volumes of poetry as well as a novel, biographies, lectures, dramas, and letters.

CARL SANDBURG (1878–1967) Sandburg first became known for his free-verse poems commemorating America and its people and places. Over a long life, he garnered two Pulitzer Prizes, including one for the second part of his celebrated biography of Abraham Lincoln.

WILLIAM SAROYAN (1908–1981) Born in Fresno, California, he was a self-educated high-school dropout who would become a celebrated short-story writer, novelist, essayist, playwright, and winner of a Pulitzer Prize. He is probably best remembered today for writing the film *The Human Comedy* (1943), the best-selling novel based on it, and the drama, *The Time of Your Life* (1939).

DELMORE SCHWARTZ (1913–1966) Much associated with literary life of New York City before and after World War II, Schwartz was a poet, short-story writer, and critic. He taught at Harvard for several years, lectured at New York University, and was an editor for both *Partisan Review* and the *New Republic*.

HORACE E. SCUDDER (1838–1902) Scudder edited the *Atlantic Monthly* during the 1890s when it was the most prestigious magazine in the United States. He was also the author of a popular series of children's books as well as biographies of Oliver Wendell Holmes, Noah Webster, and George Washington.

RICHARD SEAVER (b. 1926) Seaver was an early editor of the *Evergreen Review* and a chief editor at Grove Press for many years. He was William S. Burroughs's editor for thirty-nine years. He has translated some forty books from the French. He is currently the president of Arcade Publishing.

WALLACE STEVENS (1879–1955) Educated at Harvard and New York University Law School, Stevens had a long business career with an insurance company in Hartford, Connecticut. He first came to the attention of editor Harriet Monroe at *Poetry* magazine in 1914, but it would be almost ten years before he published his first book, *Harmonium* (1923). His second, *Ideas of Order* did not appear until 1936 when Stevens was well over fifty years old. By the time of his death, the same year his *Collected Poems* (1955) was published, he was recognized as an important American poet.

BOOTH TARKINGTON (1869–1946) The author so identified with his native Indiana wrote genial novels of life in small Midwestern towns. *Penrod* (1914), the adventures of a twelve-year-old boy, was popular for decades. However, his more mature novels, *The Magnificent Ambersons* (1918) and *Alice Adams* (1912), have proved more lasting.

ALLEN TATE (1899–1979) Tate became known as one of "the Fugitives," a group of Southern poets centered around Vanderbilt University. He was an early admirer of T. S. Eliot's work. He taught for most of his career and mentored many younger poets, such as Lowell and Jarrell. He published over two dozen works of poetry and criticism.

SARA TEASDALE (1884–1933) The author of several volumes of highly personal. lyrical poems, she won the Columbia University Poetry Society Prize (which became the Pulitzer Prize for poetry) for *Love Songs* which appeared in 1917. She committed suicide at the age of forty-eight.

HENRY DAVID THOREAU (1817–1862) After graduating from Harvard College, Thoreau returned to his native Concord, Massachusetts, where he taught school briefly before becoming a self-described "inspector of snow storms." A friend and admirer of Emerson, he became the most ardent of the Transcendentalists, renowned for his love of nature and philosophical musing. His book *Walden* (1854) is an American classic.

JAMES THURBER (1894–1961) The writer, cartoonist, and humorist grew up in Columbus, Ohio, and moved to New York where he achieved great success from his pieces that graced the pages of the *New Yorker* for more than thirty years. In 1996 the Library of America published a collection of his writings and drawings.

MARK TWAIN (1835–1910) Born Samuel Clemens in Hannibal, Missouri, Twain remains a central figure in American literature. His light and satiric approach often masks the serious social concerns that were an important part of his literary work. *The Adventures of Tom Sawyer* (1876), *Life on the Mississippi* (1883), and *The Adventures of Huckleberry Finn* (1884) are part of the American canon.

LOUIS UNTERMEYER (1885–1977) He was a poet of some distinction but is best remembered for his anthologies, including *Modern American Poetry* (1919), *Modern British Poetry* (1920), and many others, most of which were revised numerous times.

ROBERT PENN WARREN (1905–1989) Though he was highly regarded as a poet, he became better known as a novelist, especially for the Pulitzer Prize–winning *All the King's Men* (1947). In 1985 he became the first Poet Laureate of the United States.

EUDORA WELTY (1909–2001) Welty lived for most of her life in Jackson, Mississippi. Though nearly all her stories and novels are set in the Southern world of her experience, they achieve a universality beyond region. The best of her work has been collected in a two-volume Library of America edition.

E. B. WHITE (1899–1985) A stalwart of the early *New Yorker* magazine, he wrote graceful and humorous pieces that are much admired for their sytle. He also wrote stories for children, including *Charlotte's Web* (1952); revised Strunk's *The Elements of Style* (1959); and teamed up with his friend and colleague James Thurber on *Is Sex Necessary?* (1929).

JOHN GREENLEAF WHITTIER (1807–1892) The "Yankee pastoral" poet's best work appeared during and just after the Civil War, which he both criticized and celebrated in verse. The Massachusetts-born Quaker was an influential spokesman in the anti-slavery cause.

WILLIAM CARLOS WILLIAMS (1883–1963) Generally regarded as one of the most original American poets of the last century, Williams was also a practicing physician in Rutherford, New Jersey, for forty years. His most famous work is the five-volume poem *Paterson* (1946–1958).

EDMUND WILSON (1895–1972) One of the great literary critics the United States has produced, Wilson was of the same generation as Ernest Hemingway and F. Scott Fitzgerald (with whom he attended Princeton). Over the years he reviewed books for such magazines as the *New Republic*, *Vanity Fair*, and the *New Yorker*. Some of his most famous books are *Axel's Castle* (1931), *To the Finland Station* (1940), and *Patriotic Gore* (1962). His published diaries virtually present an intellectual history of twentieth-century America.

THOMAS WOLFE (1900–1938) A native of North Carolina, Wolfe, with his huge energy and ambition, wrote a series of long novels, including *Look Homeward, Angel* (1929) and *Of Time and the River* (1935). Concerned with family life in the rural South and the journey of the writer protagonist to New York, the novels parallel Wolfe's own life, including battles with his famous editor, Maxwell Perkins.

JAMES WOOD (b. 1965) Born and educated in England, Wood has lived in the U.S. since 1996. A critic, novelist, editor, and professor of literature, he wrote the introduction to Saul Bellow's *Collected Stories* (2001) and edited the first of the Bellow volumes in the Library of America series (2003).

GEORGE EDWARD WOODBERRY (1855–1931) Woodberry was a poet and literary essayist, noted as an editor of Shelley and a biographer of Poe and Hawthorne.

RICHARD WRIGHT (1908–1960) Wright's autobiography, *Black Boy* (1945), describes his childhood and youth in Mississippi before he moved to Chicago as a young man. It was there that he first began to write, publishing short stories until his novel *Native Son* (1940) made him famous. Living in France after World War II he continued to publish and was at the center of expatriate African American life in Paris.

ELINOR WYLIE (1885–1928) A poet and novelist widely read in her day, Wylie was aristocratic, scandalous, and bohemian, living in

New York's Greenwich Village in the 1920s. After leaving her first husband and divorcing her second, she married the well-known poet William Rose Benét. In the years just after World War I in New York, her work began to mature and she was greatly encouraged by the young critic Edmund Wilson.

JONATHAN YARDLEY (b. 1939) Yardley is a Pulitzer Prize-winning critic who writes about books and culture for the *Washington Post*. He is also the author of a wide range of books.

ACKNOWLEDGMENTS

Baldwin, James, "Eight Men," the first part of a three-part essay entitled "Alas, Poor Richard," was originally published in the *Reporter*, copyright © 1961 by James Baldwin. Copyright renewed. Collected in *Nobody Knows My Name*, published by Vintage Books. Reprinted by arrangement with the James Baldwin Estate.

Bellow, Saul, "John Cheever," copyright © 1983 by Saul Bellow, from *It All Adds Up* by Saul Bellow. Used by permission of Viking Penguin, a division of Penguin Putnam Inc.

Buford, Bill, "Martha Gellhorn," *Los Angeles Times Book Review* (April 1998). Copyright © 1998 by Bill Buford. Used by permission of author.

Busch, Frederick, "Andre and the Daughters," from *Andre Dubus: Tributes* (Donald Anderson, editor). Copyright © 2001 by Xavier Review Press. Used by permission of Frederick Busch.

Campbell, Wendy, "Sylvia Plath," from *The Art of Sylvia Plath: A Symposium* (Charles Newman, editor), Indiana University Press, 1970.

Creeley, Robert, "Ted Berrigan's Death," from *The Collected Essays of Robert Creeley*. Copyright © 1989 by the Regents of the University of California Press.

Davenport, Guy, "Thomas Merton R I P," *National Review* (December 31, 1968). Copyright © 1968 by National Review, Inc., 215 Lexington Avenue, New York, NY 10016. Reprinted by permission.

Di Prima, Diane, "Lust for Life," *Los Angeles Times Book Review* (May 18, 1997). Copyright © 1997 by Diane di Prima. Used by permission of the author.

Fitzgerald, F. Scott, "Ring," the *New Republic* (November 11, 1933).

Hoagland, Edward, "Standing Tough in the Desert," *New York Times Book Review* (May 7, 1989). Copyright © 1989 by the New York Times Co. Reprinted by permission.

Humphries, Rolfe, "Edna St. Vincent Millay." Reprinted with permission from the December 30, 1950, issue of the *Nation*.

ACKNOWLEDGMENTS

Jarrell, Randall, "Ernie Pyle." Reprinted with permission from the May 19, 1945 issue of the *Nation*.

Kenner, Hugh, "William Carlos Williams: In Memoriam," *National Review* (March 26, 1963). Copyright © 1963 by National Review, Inc. Reprinted by permission.

Leonard, John, "Mary McCarthy Remembered." Copyright © 1993, *The Last Innocent White Man in America and Other Writings* by John Leonard. Reprinted by permission of The New Press.

Levertov, Denise, "Muriel Rukeyser," from *Light Up the Cave*, copyright © 1981 by New Directions Publishing Corp. Reprinted by permission of New Directions Publishing Corp.

Lowell, Robert, "Randall Jarrell: 1914–1965," from *Collected Prose* by Robert Lowell. Copyright © 1987 by Caroline Lowell, Harriet Lowell, and Sheridan Lowell. Intro © 1987 by Robert Giroux. Reprinted by permission of Farrar, Straus and Giroux, LLC.

MacLeish, Archibald, "Ernest Hemingway," *Life* (July 14, 1961). Reprinted by permission.

McCarthy, Mary, "Philip Rahv," the *New York Times Book Review* (February 17, 1974). Copyright © 1974 by the New York Times Co. Reprinted by permission.

Morrison, Toni, "Life in His Language." Reprinted by permission of International Creative Management, Inc. Copyright © 1989 by Toni Morrison. Published in *James Baldwin: The Legacy* (Quincy Troupe, ed.), Simon & Schuster, 1989.

O'Hara, John, "In Memory of F. Scott Fitzgerald," the *New Republic* (March 3, 1941).

Porter, Katherine Anne, "Flannery O'Connor at Home," from *The Collected Essays and Occasional Writings of Katherine Anne Porter* (New York: Delacorte Press/Seymour Lawrence, 1970). Originally published in *Esprit* (1964). Reprinted with the permission of the Permissions Company on behalf of Barbara Thompson Davis, Literary Trustee for the Estate of Katherine Anne Porter.

Price, Reynolds, "James Dickey, Size XL," the *New York Tmes Book Review* (March 23, 1997). Copyright © 1997 by the New York Times Co. Reprinted by permission.

ACKNOWLEDGMENTS

Saroyan, William, "Carl Sandburg," from *Letters from 74 rue Taitbout, or Don't Go But If You Must Say Hello to Everybody* (1969). Permission to reprint by the Trustees of Leland Stanford Junior University.

Schwartz, Delmore, "Wallace Stevens," from the *New Republic* (August 22, 1955).

Seaver, Richard, "Rebel, Rebel," *Los Angeles Times Book Review* (August 10, 1997). Copyright © 1997 by Richard Seaver. Used by permission of author.

Tate, Allen, "Homage to T. S. Eliot." Copyright © 1966 by Allen Tate. Collected in *Memoirs and Opinions 1926–1975*, The Swallow Press, 1975.

Warrern, Robert Penn, "Katherine Anne Porter," *Proceedings of the American Academy and Institute of Arts and Letters*, 31 (1980). Reprinted by permission of the Estate of Robert Penn Warren.

White, E. B., "James Thurber." Originally published in the *New Yorker* (November 11, 1961). Reprinted by permission. Copyright © 1961 E. B. White. All rights reserved.

Wilson, Edmund, "The Death of Elinor Wylie," from *The Shores of Light: A Literary Chronicle of the Twenties and Thirties* by Edmund Wilson. Copyright © 1952 by Edmund Wilson. Copyright © renewed 1980 by Helen Miranda Wilson. Reprinted by permission of Farrar, Straus and Giroux, LLC.

Wood, James, "Gratitude" (Saul Bellow), *The New Republic* (April 25, 2005). Copyright © 2005 by the *New Republic*. Reprinted by permission of James Wood.

Yardley, Jonathan, "Eudora Welty," *Washington Post* (July 30, 2001). Copyright © 2001 by the *Washington Post*. Reprinted with permission.